Cambridge F

C000128711

Elements in Ep
edited by
Stephen Hetherington
University of New South Wales, Sydney

WISDOM

A Skill Theory

Cheng-hung Tsai
Institute of European and American Studies,
Academia Sinica

CAMBRIDGE
UNIVERSITY PRESS

CAMBRIDGE
UNIVERSITY PRESS

Shaftesbury Road, Cambridge CB2 8EA, United Kingdom

One Liberty Plaza, 20th Floor, New York, NY 10006, USA

477 Williamstown Road, Port Melbourne, VIC 3207, Australia

314–321, 3rd Floor, Plot 3, Splendor Forum, Jasola District Centre,
New Delhi – 110025, India

103 Penang Road, #05–06/07, Visioncrest Commercial, Singapore 238467

Cambridge University Press is part of Cambridge University Press & Assessment,
a department of the University of Cambridge.

We share the University's mission to contribute to society through the pursuit of
education, learning and research at the highest international levels of excellence.

www.cambridge.org
Information on this title: www.cambridge.org/9781009222891

DOI: 10.1017/9781009222884

First published 2022

A catalogue record for this publication is available from the British Library.

ISBN 978-1-009-22289-1 Paperback
ISSN 2398-0567 (online)
ISSN 2514-3832 (print)

Cambridge University Press & Assessment has no responsibility for the persistence
or accuracy of URLs for external or third-party internet websites referred to in this
publication and does not guarantee that any content on such websites is, or will
remain, accurate or appropriate.

Wisdom

A Skill Theory

Elements in Epistemology

DOI: 10.1017/9781009222884
First published online: December 2022

Cheng-hung Tsai
Institute of European and American Studies, Academia Sinica

Author for correspondence: Cheng-hung Tsai, chtsai917@gate.sinica.edu.tw

Abstract: What is wisdom? What does a wise person know? Can a wise person know how to act and live well without knowing the whys and wherefores of his or her own action? How is wisdom acquired? This Element addresses questions regarding the nature and acquisition of wisdom by developing and defending a skill theory of wisdom. Specifically, this theory argues that if a person S is wise, then (i) S knows that overall attitude success contributes to or constitutes well-being; (ii) S knows what the best means to achieve well-being are; (iii) S is reliably successful at acting and living well (in light of what S knows); and (iv) S knows why he or she is successful at acting and living well. The first three sections of this Element develop this theory, and the final two sections defend this theory against two objections to the effect that there are asymmetries between wisdom and skill.

Keywords: wisdom, skill, knowing how, deliberation, well-being

ISBNs: 9781009222891 (PB), 9781009222884 (OC)
ISSNs: 2398-0567 (online), 2514-3832 (print)

Contents

Introduction

Wisdom has been highly praised by philosophers, psychologists, politicians, religious leaders, poets, and the general public.[1] Wisdom is assumed to be something the possession of which enables one to deliberate, act, and live well. However, what exactly is this "something"? And if there is such a thing, how can we human beings acquire and maintain it?

According to the view held by philosophers (e.g., Nozick 1989; Tiberius 2008; Swartwood 2013; Grimm 2015) and psychologists (e.g., Baltes and Staudinger 2000; Sternberg 2001),[2] a person S is wise if and only if S knows how to live well. This view highlights two features of wisdom: first, wisdom is concerned with well-being; second, wisdom is a kind of knowledge-how. But what is such knowledge-how like? Is it a skill, or a knack? What does a wise person know about well-being? What kind of theory can be developed from the view that wisdom is knowing how to live well? What difficulties does a knowing-how view of wisdom encounter? Philosophers and psychologists have not yet brought these issues and problems to the fore and dealt with them in a systematic way. For example, psychologists who view wisdom as skill do not recognize the theoretical difficulties in conceptualizing wisdom as skill (such as the objections addressed in Sections 4 and 5 of this Element). Philosophers who view wisdom as skill keep the issue about what a wise person knows about well-being as implicit as possible, and tell us little about how wisdom can be learned and improved *as a skill*. This Element aims to develop and defend a theory of wisdom – the *expertise theory* of wisdom – in a systematic manner and by reference to contemporary studies of knowledge-how, skill, and expertise.

This Element consists of three parts. Part I, "A Skill Theory of Wisdom Presented," consists of one section (Section 1), which details the motivations and arguments underlying the skill model of wisdom and proposes a version of the skill model.

Part II, "The Theory Developed," consists of two sections. To examine the nature of wisdom qua skill more deeply and to develop the expertise theory of wisdom presented in Section 1, we address two issues in this context.

The first issue pertains to whether wisdom requires articulacy, that is, whether a wise person qua an expert is required to possess an articulate skill that takes his

---

[1] It is often assumed that there are two distinct kinds of wisdom: theoretical wisdom (*sophia*) and practical wisdom (*phronesis*). However, Jason Baehr (2012) argues that this distinction is not as sharp as some philosophers believe. In this Element, this issue is left aside, and the term "wisdom" is always used to refer to practical wisdom unless otherwise noted.

[2] According to psychologists Ferrari and Kim, "[a]lthough there are many definitions of wisdom, we find a surprising consensus in the scientific literature. At the most general level, this consensus is well-summarized by Grimm (2015), for whom wisdom concerns knowledge of how to live the best life" (Ferrari and Kim 2019: 347).

or her practical skill of living as its object of explanation. To address this issue, we discuss two competing accounts of expertise in Section 2 and argue for a perspective that views wisdom as exhibiting two levels: a combination of a first-order practical skill and a second-order articulate skill.

The second issue pertains to the content of wisdom, in particular to what is known by a wise person regarding well-being. Section 3 develops a fully articulated theory of wisdom by integrating the expertise theory of wisdom (in its partially articulated form) with the *success theory of well-being*, arguing that wisdom is a (complex) skill that is conducive to well-being, which is conceived of in terms of overall attitude success.

Part III, "The Theory Defended," consists of two sections. The preceding sections establish the expertise theory of wisdom, which exemplifies a skill model of wisdom. However, two types of objections can be raised to the skill model of wisdom in general and the expertise theory of wisdom in particular.

The first type of objection argues that certain distinct features are present in wisdom but not in skill. A special case of this type of objection is the claim that a person with wisdom can and should deliberate about the (final) end being pursued, but a person with a particular skill cannot deliberate about the (final) end of that skill (and even if he or she can, he or she is not required to do so). I call this the Deliberation Objection. Section 4 aims to respond to the Deliberation Objection by showing how an expert in a field can and should deliberate about the end being pursued.

The second type of objection argues that certain distinct features are present in skill but not in wisdom. A special case of this type of objection is the claim that skill has sufficient feedback for learning and improvement, but wisdom has no such feedback. I call this the Feedback Objection. Section 5 aims to respond to the Feedback Objection by showing that the argument for it is not as sound as it appears to be. The underlying aim of Section 5 is to illustrate the way in which wisdom can be acquired.

Part I   A Skill Theory of Wisdom Presented

1 Wisdom as Knowing How to Live Well

1.1 The Skill Model of Wisdom in Philosophy

A wise person *knows how* to live well. Such know-how involves a special kind of practical reasoning – *good reasoning* regarding how to live well (happily or virtuously). Contemporary philosophers have contributed to the development of the skill model of wisdom, according to which the distinctive features of wisdom (or the practical reasoning of a prudent or virtuous person) can be explicated in terms of the distinctive features of skill (*techne* or expertise).[3]

There are several merits of the skill model of wisdom. The first is that the concept of wisdom, which might seem elusive to us at the outset, can be approached by means of the concept of skill, a concept with which we are more or less familiar. The second merit is that the skill model of wisdom can be empirically grounded with the aid of empirical, scientific studies of skill acquisition and expert performance.[4] An empirically grounded theory of wisdom, if correctly constructed, can "[yield] a viable epistemology in which moral knowledge is shown to be a species of a general kind of knowledge that is not philosophically suspect" (Bloomfield 2000: 23), or "give us insight into the development of virtue" (Stichter 2007: 184). The third merit is that the skill model of wisdom has the capacity to *guide* rather than merely to explain human life, although the skill model also acknowledges Robert Nozick's (1989: 270) claim that "[w]isdom does not guarantee success in achieving life's important goals, however, just as a high probability does not guarantee truth." For the skill model, wisdom, like skill, does not guarantee certain success but merely reliable success.

Some terminological and conceptual issues must be addressed at this point to avoid unnecessary worry and confusion. First, advocates of the skill model use somewhat different terms to express their views: "the skill analogy for *virtue*" (Annas 1993, 1995), "the skill model of *virtue*" (Stichter 2007), and "the expert skill model of *wisdom*" (Swartwood 2013). Some might worry that the subject matter of the skill models proposed by these authors differs: for Annas and Stichter, the subject matter is moral virtue, while for Swartwood, the subject matter is wisdom. In one respect, their models focus on a nearly identical object: The object that Annas and Stichter attempt to model by the concept of skill is good *practical reasoning* in the context of a virtuous life, and the object that Swartwood attempts to model is good *practical reasoning* in the context of a good life. Thus, although some philosophers use the term "skill model of *virtue*," this term can be treated as an abbreviation for the phrase "the skill model of *good practical reasoning* in virtue," whose main conception (i.e., good practical reasoning) is closely linked to wisdom.[5]

---

[3] Such philosophers include Annas (1995, 2011a); Bloomfield (2000, 2001, 2014); Hursthouse (2006); Stichter (2007, 2018); Russell (2009, 2012); Swartwood (2013); Tsai (2016, 2020, 2022a); and Swartwood and Tiberius (2019).

[4] For empirical studies of expertise, see Ericsson et al. (2006).

[5] Although there is reason to separate the skill model of *virtue* from the skill model of *wisdom* (this reason, briefly stated, is that wisdom is not skill because the goal of wisdom is vague or contentious; see Jacobson [2005] and Stichter [2018]; and for a critical discussion, see Section 5.4), this reason does not affect our use of the theoretical resources of the skill model

Second, to be clear, I distinguish three different understandings of the thesis that wisdom is skill: First, wisdom is identical to skill (which I call the Identity Thesis); second, wisdom is analogous to skill (which I call the Analogy Thesis);[6] and third, wisdom is a species of skill (which I call the Species Thesis). The Identity Thesis is too strong because it stipulates that all instances of skill should be treated as instances of wisdom. As we know, there are putative instances of skill that are not instances of wisdom. The Analogy Thesis is too modest because it does not provide or imply any ontological status for wisdom. The notion of analogy – such as in the context of the city–soul analogy in Plato's *Republic* – conveys no ontological import from source objects to target objects.[7] The skill model of wisdom that I develop and defend in this Element endorses the Species Thesis. That said, I nevertheless draw on resources from the Identity Thesis and the Analogy Thesis to highlight and justify certain ideas that are shared by all skill models of wisdom (for example, the merits mentioned above are shared by all skill models of wisdom).

1.2 The Skill Model of Wisdom in Psychology

One motivation for engaging with the skill model of wisdom in philosophy is that this model can serve as a conceptual foundation for the skill model of wisdom in psychology. Paul Bloomfield observes that "[a]lthough it is uncommon for philosophers today to think of the virtues as skill, ... there is good evidence from empirical psychology that supports this thinking, about wisdom in particular" (Bloomfield 2014: 225). He mentions the works of Paul Baltes and Ursula Staudinger, who propose the Berlin wisdom paradigm, which defines wisdom as "expertise in the fundamental pragmatics of life" (Baltes and Staudinger 2000),[8] as well as the work of Robert Sternberg, who proposes the balance theory of wisdom, which defines wisdom as "the application of successful intelligence and creativity as mediated by values toward the

---

of virtue to discuss and develop the skill model of wisdom. The ultimate goal of virtue, in fact, can be the same as the goal of wisdom, that is, to live a good life. So, the goal of virtue is vague as well. If virtue, so understood, can be a skill, so can wisdom. Thus, either both virtue and wisdom are skills or neither are.

[6] Compare Annas's formulation of the analogy: "The idea that the practical reasoning of the virtuous person shares important features with that of the expert in a practical skill is often referred to simply as the skill analogy" (Annas 2011a: 2).

[7] However, for Annas, "Some readers may come to think that 'analogy' is not the best term for a relation so close that some have come to think of virtue as itself being a kind of skill; but what is most important is to bring out the shared features and their importance" (Annas 2011a: 2).

[8] According to the Berlin wisdom paradigm, "Wisdom-related knowledge and skills can be characterized by a family of five criteria: (1) rich factual knowledge about life, (2) rich procedural knowledge about life, (3) life span contextualism, (4) value relativism, and (5) awareness and management of uncertainty" (Staudinger 2010: 1861).

achievement of a common good through a balance among (a) intrapersonal, (b) interpersonal, and (c) extrapersonal interests" (Sternberg 2003: 152). Both the Berlin wisdom paradigm and the balance theory of wisdom can be classified as examples of the skill model of wisdom because they view wisdom as a kind of expertise or intelligence.

What can the skill model of wisdom in philosophy contribute to the skill model of wisdom in psychology? Psychologists Sternberg and Glück believe that "it would be a serious mistake to leave the study of wisdom exclusively to philosophers (and in fact, even fewer philosophers than psychologists actually study wisdom nowadays!)," but they also claim that "[p]sychology as well as philosophy has a great deal to contribute to the study of wisdom. The philosophical and psychological approaches are complementary, with each providing insights that the other would be likely to miss" (Sternberg and Glück 2019: 787). Sternberg and Glück do not identify the element that is supposed to be missing from psychology. However, philosophers might have something to say regarding this lack.

The implicit-theories approach and the explicit-theories approach are two methodological approaches in psychology to understanding "intelligence," "creativity," and "wisdom." Implicit theories in general, according to Sternberg, "are constructions by people (whether psychologists or laypersons) that reside in the minds of these individuals. Such theories need to be discovered rather than invented because they already exist, in some form, in people's heads" (Sternberg 1985: 608). In contrast, explicit theories in general "are constructions of psychologists or other scientists that are based on or at least tested on data collected from people performing tasks presumed to measure psychological functioning" (Sternberg 1985: 607). Applying to the psychology of wisdom, "implicit theories of wisdom are the conceptions of wisdom that laypersons hold, and explicit theories of wisdom are those that are constructed and tested by psychologists and other experts" (Bluck and Glück 2005: 90).

Regarding the implicit-theoretical approach to wisdom, which searches for and studies laypersons' conceptions of wisdom, John Kekes complains that

> no scientists, jurists, or historians would dream of answering difficult questions in their field by asking randomly selected people ... People who know take it for granted that difficult questions have difficult answers and that randomly selected people lack the knowledge even to understand the difficulties involved in the questions let alone give reasonable answers to them. But psychologists assume that randomly selected people can tell what wisdom is. In nothing I have read is this assumption stated or justified. (Kekes 2020: 50)

Swartwood and Tiberius agree with Kekes since they claim that "implicit theories of wisdom on their own will not provide us with a plausible account of wisdom" (Swartwood and Tiberius 2019: 20).[9]

It is obvious that implicit theories of wisdom are not argument-driven but rather data-driven; they are concerned with what people believe about wisdom, regardless of whether these beliefs are justified. In my view, explicit theories of wisdom too may not be entirely argument-driven, because they can be overridden by implicit theories of wisdom (cf. the following: "Still, an explicit theory of wisdom that was totally inconsistent with laypeople's understanding of the term would be hard to defend" [Bluck and Glück 2005: 91]). Neither the implicit-theories approach nor the explicit-theories approach to wisdom *aims to* address such reason-demanding questions; both approaches are designed to be more data-driven than argument-driven.

If examples of the skill model of wisdom in psychology, such as the Berlin wisdom paradigm and the balance theory, are methodologically founded upon the implicit-theories and the explicit-theories approaches, they have conceptual deficiencies. The skill model of wisdom in philosophy can be a conceptual foundation for the psychology of wisdom because the former aims to explore the fundamental conceptual issues that any particular skill model of wisdom must eventually encounter, including issues such as why and whether wisdom is skill, why rich knowledge (whether propositional or procedural) is necessary for expertise and wisdom, and why and whether wisdom is anti-wicked, and so on (as readers will see in this Element). These "why" questions about wisdom – or, to put it more generally, reason-demanding questions about wisdom – lie outside the scope of the psychology of wisdom. For example, the skill model of wisdom in psychology does not recognize, let alone respond to, the serious objections against the thesis that wisdom is skill, such as the Deliberation Objection and the Feedback Objection, which are addressed in Sections 4 and 5 of this Element.

1.3 Arguments for the Skill Model of Wisdom

The skill model of wisdom treats wisdom as skill or expertise in living well. Different scholars prefer different labels,[10] formulations, or arguments for the idea that wisdom is skill. The issue of why these scholars prefer one over the

---

[9] The reason given by these authors is similar to that given by Kekes: "Lay people's views of physical laws may be unlikely to be entirely wrong, and a physical theory that was totally inconsistent with them would probably be hard to defend, but that doesn't do much to show that physicists should start their research by surveying lay views" (Swartwood and Tiberius 2019: 19).

[10] Such labels include the "skill analogy of virtue," the "skill model of virtue," and the "expert skill model of wisdom," as mentioned in Section 1.1.

other is not the main concern here. My aim is to construct an argument that is sufficiently general or abstract to highlight the relationship or connection between wisdom and skill. Consider the following argument:

The General Argument

(P1) A person S is wise if and only if S knows how to live well.

(P2) S knows how to live well if and only if S has skill or expertise in living well.

(C) S is wise if and only if S has skill or expertise in living well.

Let us call this the *General Argument* for the skill model of wisdom. This argument is valid, but its two premises require further explanation.

The view of wisdom stated in (P1) is justified by its being a meaning stipulation. According to Sharon Ryan, "This view captures Aristotle's basic idea of practical wisdom. It also captures an important aspect of views defended by Nozick, Plato, Garrett, Kekes, Maxwell, Ryan, and Tiberius" (Ryan 2013). I leave the exegesis of these philosophers to Ryan and move on to an issue that she views as difficult (cf. her claim that "an account of what it means to *know how to live well* may prove as difficult a topic as providing an account of wisdom" [Ryan 2013; emphasis mine]): If practical wisdom is knowing how to live well, then what is such knowledge-how?

Fortunately, contemporary epistemology offers resources that allow us to address this issue. According to intellectualism, knowledge-how is a species of knowledge-that (e.g., Stanley and Williamson 2001; Stanley 2011). In contrast, according to anti-intellectualism, knowledge-how is not knowledge-that but is a species of capacity or skill (e.g., Ryle 1949; Hetherington 2011, 2021).[11] At first glance, the view stated in (P2) is inclined toward anti-intellectualism. That said, we should be cautious because there are more sophisticated forms of intellectualism and anti-intellectualism about knowledge-how. For example, the notions of skill or expertise expressed in (P2) can be explained with an intellectualist flavor.[12]

---

[11] The account of knowing-how that I endorse in this Element is *Rylean* anti-intellectualism, which is an upgraded or reinterpreted version of Ryle's anti-intellectualism. According to the Rylean account, knowing-how is a hybrid skill, which is a combination of a first-order practical skill and a second-order intellectual skill. The Rylean account does not disregard the importance of propositional knowledge in a particular instance of know-how. Such propositional knowledge can be used to explain the normative and agential aspects of intelligent action. However, the Rylean account does not treat propositional knowledge as intelligence per se but rather as the *product* of exercising (second-order intellectual) intelligence. Thus construed, the Rylean account of knowing-how, which accommodates the intellectual element of intellectualism, remains anti-intellectualist. For a more detailed argument for the Rylean account, see Tsai (2014).

[12] With regard to the notion of skill or expertise with an intellectualist flavor, see Annas (2011a, 2011b) and Montero (2016).

In the philosophical literature, other arguments have been created to support the skill model of wisdom, such as Jason Swartwood's (2013) "Core Argument," which is more complicated than the General Argument. However, the Core Argument can be simplified and reconstructed as follows:

The Simplified Core Argument
(P1) Wisdom is knowing how to live well in the sense of knowing how to conduct oneself.

(P2) Knowing how to conduct oneself is an expert decision-making skill, which is composed of a set of five subskills (intuition, deliberation, metacognition, self-regulation, and self-cultivation).

(C) Wisdom is an expert decision-making skill.

The Simplified Core Argument mirrors the main structure of the General Argument. Details and objections aside, the General Argument, or something like it, can help us understand how and why wisdom can be related to skill.

1.4 The Expertise Theory of Wisdom

1.4.1 Two Characters

Knowing-how, skill, and expertise are goal-oriented. A person with a particular skill or an expert in a particular field can be seen as a person equipped with a sort of particular goal-oriented system, which enables and requires the person to know what he or she, qua an expert in that field, exactly and ultimately should achieve in the field when exercising the skill, and what the best or effective means are to achieve it. Thus, assuming that wisdom is skill or expertise in living well, a wise person knows not only what well-being is but also what the best means or strategies are to achieve it. To put this view more formally:

> *The goal-oriented character of wisdom qua skill*: A person S is wise (i.e., S knows how to live well, or S has skill or expertise in living well) only if (i) S knows what contributes to or constitutes well-being, and (ii) S knows what the best means to achieve well-being are.

This view echoes and *justifies* the views of wisdom espoused by Grimm and Nozick. In his article "Wisdom," Grimm lists three necessary conditions for knowing how to live well:

> On my view knowledge of how to live well is a complex state that can be broken down into various components. In particular, knowing how to live well is constituted by the following further types of knowledge, all of

which ... are individually necessary for wisdom: (1) Knowledge of what is good or important for well-being. (2) Knowledge of one's standing relative to what is good or important for well-being. (3) Knowledge of a strategy for obtaining what is good or important for well-being. (Grimm 2015: 139–140)

In a chapter of his *The Examined Life*, "What Is Wisdom and Why Do Philosophers Love It So?," Nozick lists several elements of wisdom:

What a wise person needs to know and understand constitutes a varied list: the most important goals and values of life – the ultimate goal, if there is one; what means will reach these goals without too great a cost; what kinds of dangers threaten the achieving of these goals; how to recognize and avoid or minimize these dangers; what different types of human beings are like in their actions and motives (as this presents dangers or opportunities); what is not possible or feasible to achieve (or avoid); how to tell what is appropriate when; knowing when certain goals are sufficiently achieved; what limitations are unavoidable and how to accept them; how to improve oneself and one's relationships with others or society; knowing what the true and unapparent value of various things is; when to take a long-term view; knowing the variety and obduracy of facts, institutions, and human nature; understanding what one's real motives are; how to cope and deal with the major tragedies and dilemmas of life, and with the major good things too. (Nozick 1989: 269)

In Grimm's list, the first and third types of knowledge are knowledge about goals and knowledge about means, respectively. In Nozick's list, knowledge about the first two items is clearly knowledge about goals and knowledge about means. The second type of knowledge in Grimm's list as well as most items in Nozick's list, other than the first two, can be seen as the sort of information that is necessary for or beneficial to knowledge about means, that is, information that helps the subject in question figure out what the best means or strategies to achieve well-being are. Both Grimm and Nozick attribute the goal-oriented character to wisdom, although they do not proclaim the skill model of wisdom.

Another character that wisdom can inherit from know-how, skill, or expertise is the success-conducive character. A person is unlikely to be qualified as an expert in a particular field if the person cannot successfully achieve the goal in that field. For example, a person who, after trying, does not have mobility in aquatic environments is not a swimmer in a normal sense, even if the person has all the propositional knowledge that Michael Phelps has about swimming. (The person might be an expert in *teaching* others how to swim, but this is not the goal of the swimming skill.) Thus, assuming that wisdom is skill or expertise in living well, a person with wisdom must successfully achieve well-being. Let us formulate the view as follows:

The success-conducive character of wisdom qua skill: A person S is wise only if S is reliably successful at acting and living well.

This view of wisdom also echoes and *justifies* certain philosophers' views of wisdom. For example, according to Sharon Ryan,

> Philosophers who are attracted to the idea that knowing how to live well is a necessary condition for wisdom might want to simply tack on a success condition to (KLW) [i.e., S is wise iff S knows how to live well] to get around cases in which a person knows all about living well, yet fails to put this knowledge into practice. Something along the lines of the following theory would capture this idea.
>
> *Wisdom as Knowing How to, and Succeeding at, Living Well (KLS):*
> S is wise iff (i) S knows how to live well, and (ii) S is successful at living well.
>
> The idea of the success condition is that one puts one's knowledge into practice. (Ryan 2013)

Aligning with the proponents of (KLS) stated in the above passage, Grimm adds an application condition to his view of wisdom mentioned earlier:

> Notice that I have claimed only that our conditions on wisdom are individually necessary, not jointly sufficient; so it remains to be determined what else needs to be added in order to complete or round out the view. By my lights, the main obvious contender is some sort of application condition: that the wise person not only knows what is good or important for well-being and has effective strategies for achieving these goods, but actually *does* achieve these goods. (Grimm 2015: 152–153)

Philosophers attribute the success-conducive character to wisdom, although they do not explicitly proclaim the skill model of wisdom, let alone justify their conception of wisdom by the characters of skill and expertise.

1.4.2 The Theory

Based on what has been said above, a version of the skill model of wisdom, which I shall call the "expertise theory" of wisdom, can be formulated as follows:

The Expertise Theory of Wisdom, v.1
(T1) S is wise if and only if S has skill or expertise in living well.
(T2) S is wise only if

> (i)   S knows what contributes to or constitutes well-being;
> (ii) S knows what the best means to achieve well-being are; and
> (iii) S is reliably successful at acting and living well (in light of what S knows).

The expertise theory of wisdom *v.1* is composed of two theses: (T1) is supported by the General Argument; (T2-i) and (T2-ii) state the goal-oriented character of wisdom qua skill, which is supported by (T1) and the goal-oriented character of *skill*; (T2-iii) states the success-conducive character of wisdom qua skill, which is supported by (T1) and the success-conducive character of *skill*.

Note that at this stage, the expertise theory of wisdom *v.1* remains a *partially articulated* theory of wisdom (as will be explained in Section 1.5) because its atomic clause (i) does not tell us what is actually known by S regarding what it *is* that contributes to or constitutes well-being.

1.5 Partially versus Fully Articulated Theories of Wisdom

Philosophers often say that a person is wise only if they know what matters for well-being, what is important for well-being, or what it is worthwhile to pursue. The question that remains is: What is it that matters for well-being? Or, what *is* important for well-being? Or, what *is* a worthwhile end to pursue? Not all theories of wisdom address such questions. Using Grimm's terminologies, a theory of wisdom is *fully articulated* "if it not only invokes notions like 'what is important for well-being' but also tells us what *is* important for well-being"; such a theory will opt for a "particular view about what is more or less important for well-being, or about what is most important, or about how broadly the notion of well-being should be understood" (Grimm 2015: 142). Otherwise, a theory of wisdom is *partially articulated*. The expertise theory of wisdom *v.1*, in its current form, is a *partially articulated* theory of wisdom.

In the wisdom literature, philosophers either leave the above question aside (that is, they are satisfied with or limited to partially articulated theories of wisdom) or presuppose, whether implicitly or explicitly, a particular conception of well-being without considering the philosophical debates about well-being. In the latter case, philosophers often attribute the Aristotelian conception of well-being to a wise person. However, *eudaimonism* is just one of many theories of well-being. Why are hedonism or informed desire theories not taken into consideration? Is it because *eudaimonism* is the only theory of well-being that can fit a theory of wisdom? (If so, can we thus exclude all other alternative theories of well-being because the conceptions of a good life they offer are not of the sort of life that a wise person would recognize as good?)

At any rate, a fully articulated theory of wisdom has more theoretical virtue and practical merit than a partially articulated theory, which can never be tested seriously or used in practice. With regard to the theoretical dimension, a fully articulated theory of wisdom can be more testable (or falsifiable) because it is more substantial. With regard to the practical dimension, a fully articulated theory of wisdom, if it is correct, can be used to guide a person who wants to be wise or who wants to identify or determine an exemplar of wisdom.

How can we construct a fully articulated theory of wisdom? In principle, we can combine any partially articulated theory of wisdom with any theory of well-being (see Section 3.2). Therefore, there are many possible fully articulated theories of wisdom. However, being a possible theory is one thing, and being a reasonable theory is quite another.

The expertise theory of wisdom *v.1* can be developed into a better fully articulated theory. In Section 2, I will consider whether the expertise theory of wisdom *v.1*, as a partially articulated theory, is good enough for a skill model of wisdom. In Section 3, I will make possible and sensible a fully articulated theory of wisdom that integrates the expertise theory of wisdom with the *success theory* of well-being.

Part II The Theory Developed

2 Wisdom and Knowing the Whys

2.1 The Issue

According to the expertise theory of wisdom *v.1*, a wise person S is reliably successful at acting and living well. Suppose that S is successful at acting well in a certain circumstance. Is S required to have the skill to explain and defend his or her acting in a certain way rather than otherwise? Or to put it in a more epistemological vein, can S, as a wise person, know how to act and live well without knowing the whys and wherefores of his or her own action?[13]

Why is this an issue for the skill model of wisdom? Briefly speaking, if knowing-how is fundamental to the skill model of wisdom, then the issue of whether knowing-how requires knowing the whys and wherefores is crucial to the skill model. Julia Annas and Matt Stichter are two prominent advocates of the skill model of virtuous agency.[14] However, their views about virtuous agency diverge when delving into the nature of skill (*at the level of expertise*). Annas endorses the view that a skill requires articulacy in the sense that an expert in a skill is required to have an ability to "give an account,"[15] explaining and

---

[13] Here I assume that S knows why p iff there exists some q such that S knows that *p because q*, or that *q explains why p*, or that *q is the explanation of p*.

[14] Annas attributes the skill model to Plato (or, more accurately, Plato's Socrates) while Stichter attributes the skill model to Aristotle. An exegetical issue is raised here: Annas claims that Aristotle rejects the skill model altogether (Annas 1995: 228, 2003: 16), but Stichter (2007: 189–190) insists that Aristotle does endorse the skill model and accuses Annas of mischaracterizing Aristotle's position on it due to ignoring that there is a different version of the skill model from Annas's own. The exegetical issue of whether Aristotle endorses the skill model (see, e.g., Angier 2010; Stalnaker 2010) is left aside in this Element.

[15] Compare: "The ability to 'give an account' of something is associated with the possession of *techne* from the earliest dialogues of Plato" (Nightingale 2004: 109).

defending one's exercise of the skill (let us call it "the articulacy requirement"). Contrary to Annas, Stichter denies the articulacy requirement because he thinks that it "is something that Annas assumes, rather than argues" and that Annas "is advancing an account of skills that does not fit numerous examples of actual skills" (Stichter 2007: 187). When applying these two competitive views of skill to wisdom, two views about wisdom emerge and diverge. One view holds that wisdom requires "giving an account" or knowing the whys, whereas the other denies this requirement. The following questions then arise: Which view of skill is correct? and Which view of skill best characterizes wisdom?

To make clear what is at issue, we can highlight two types of skills (or abilities) to which the articulacy requirement refers: one is a particular *practical* skill, such as driving, swimming, or farming, and another is an articulate skill, that is, the skill in articulating the underlying and unifying principles which define the practical skill in question.[16] The key to the articulacy requirement is that it asserts that a mere practical skill is insufficient for skill *at the level of expertise*; an extra articulate skill is required. For those who endorse the articulacy requirement, skill at the level of expertise is a combination of a first-order practical skill and a second-order articulate skill that takes the first-order skill (and its performance) as its object of examination, explanation, or evaluation. The controversial issue over the articulacy requirement lies in whether this extra second-order articulate skill is required for expertise, or whether a mere practical skill is sufficient.

In what follows we will consider a critical dialectic between the objections to the articulacy requirement (Section 2.2 and Section 2.4) and the replies to the objections (Section 2.3 and Section 2.5). This consideration helps us to see why a new argument for the articulacy requirement is needed as well as what kind of argument is required.

2.2 Two Objections to the Articulacy Requirement

According to Annas, there are three necessary conditions (elements or components) for skill or expertise: "It must be teachable; it must involve a unified grasp of the general principles holding of the field in question; and it must involve an articulate ability to explain and defend the particular judgments and decisions that are made" (Annas 1995: 233; see also Annas 2001: 244–245, 2003: 17–18). Annas occasionally integrates the last two conditions into one condition, expressed as follows: "The condition being spelled out here is that the person with a skill be able explicitly to explain and justify her particular

---

[16] Although Annas uses the terms "articulate ability," "rational ability," and "ability to give an account" interchangeably in her works, I primarily use the term "articulate skill" in this Element.

decisions and judgments, and to do so in terms of some general grasp of the principles which define that skill" (Annas 1995: 233). That is, what is and should be articulated by an expert is about, and depends on, what is comprehensively grasped by the expert in mastering a skill.

Stichter understands Annas as claiming that "[g]enuine skills, on the intellectualist view, require a profound understanding of their subject matter and of the underlying principles of the skill" (Stichter 2007: 188), and he disagrees with such a requirement because it "form[s] a high intellectual standard for skills that strikes people as counterintuitive" (Stichter 2007: 186). Contrary to Annas's account, Stichter thinks that the empiricist account of skill or expertise, especially the version famously developed by Hubert Dreyfus and Stuart Dreyfus (1986, 1991), is more intuitive and empirically grounded. According to Hubert and Stuart Dreyfus:

> It seems that beginners make judgments using strict rules and features, but that with talent and a great deal of involved experience the beginner develops into an expert who sees intuitively what to do without applying rules and making judgments at all. The intellectualist tradition has given an accurate description of the beginner and the expert facing an unfamiliar situation, but normally an expert does not solve problems. He does not reason. He does not even act deliberately. Rather he spontaneously does what has normally worked and, naturally, it normally works.
> (Dreyfus and Dreyfus 1991: 235; cited by Stichter 2007: 191–192)

An expert does not apply rules or act deliberately, let alone be able to articulate what the rules are that underlie his or her skill.[17]

In addition to appealing to Dreyfus and Dreyfus's account of skill, Stichter raises two objections to Annas's account, which are encapsulated in the following passage:

> That there are skills that display the three intellectual components, however, is something that Annas assumes, rather than argues. A comparison of virtues to skills will be illuminating only insofar as we are dealing with an accurate account of the acquisition of skills. Annas should be more concerned about the fact that she is advancing an account of skills that does not fit numerous examples of actual skills. If there are no skills that contain these strong intellectual components, then Socrates' account of virtue ceases to be on a par with practical skills. Annas owes an argument for the claim that there are such skills, especially since she comes up with numerous examples of skills that do not fit the Socratic conception, but almost none that do fit the conception. (Stichter 2007: 187–188)

---

[17] Gardening, sports skills, and nursing skills (e.g., Benner 2001: Ch. 2) are often used as examples of skills without articulacy.

Two objections can be extracted from this passage, which I shall call the *no-argument objection* and the *counterexample objection*. The first, the no-argument objection, says that a proponent of the articulacy requirement must tell us what his or her argument is, what the reason is for supporting the requirement; however, Annas provides no argument for the requirement. Regardless of whether or not an argument is given, the second, the counter-example objection, says that a correct account of the nature of expertise must resist counterexample; however, Annas's account of expertise, which endorses the articulacy requirement, faces counterexamples.

2.3 Two Arguments for the Articulacy Requirement

2.3.1 The Skill/Knack Distinction

Does Annas give no argument for the articulacy requirement, but just assume its correctness? I think she does offer (albeit implicitly) an argument for the articulacy requirement in her early and later works (Annas 1995, 2001, 2011a, 2011b). Her argument exploits an intuitive contrast between skills (or expertise) and knacks (or routine habits).

What is it that distinguishes skill from knack? In "Virtue as a Skill," Annas writes, "This is even more true of Socrates' most important claim about skills, namely that what distinguishes a skill from a mere knack is an ability to 'give an account' (*logon didonai*)" (Annas 1995: 232). And in "Moral Knowledge as Practical Knowledge," Annas addresses the distinction between practical knack and practical expertise as follows:

> Either "knowing how" involves "knowing that" or it does not. If it does not, then what we think of as practical knowledge is being construed as a kind of inarticulate practical knack, an ability to manipulate the world which is not at a sufficiently rational level to be judged epistemically. This, however, would amount to saying that there is no such thing as practical expertise, only knacks – that there is no significant difference between the inarticulate practitioner and the expert in the field. This is ridiculous. (Annas 2001: 248).[18]

Briefly, Annas treats one's ability to give an account, or to articulate or explain why he or she does what he or she does as an essential feature that distinguishes skill (or expertise) from knack. This treatment constitutes the core

---

[18] Annas's statement that "Either 'knowing how' involves 'knowing that' or it does not" can be read more charitably as saying that "Either 'knowing how to do something' involves 'knowing that such-and-such is an underlying principle upon which one acts' or it does not." Otherwise, the term "knowing that" might be read as referring to any kind of propositional knowledge whatsoever.

of Annas's argument for the articulacy requirement, which now can be formulated as follows:

(P1) If articulacy is what distinguishes skill (or expertise) from knack, then articulacy is a component of skill (or expertise) but not of knack.

(P2) Articulacy is what distinguishes skill (or expertise) from knack.

(C) Thus, articulacy is a component of skill (or expertise) but not knack.

The antecedent of (P1) presupposes a phenomenon to be explained (i.e., there *is* a distinction between skill and knack) and suggests an explanans (i.e., articulacy). (P1) also assumes that what is necessary to distinguish X from Y is what constitutes X. I believe that the above argument is the argument to which Annas appeals in supporting the articulacy requirement, although merely having an argument does not mean that the argument is correct.

2.3.2 Two Notions of "Expertise"

Annas is very aware of the counterexample objection; as she says, "it is clear that this idea –that a skill involve a rational ability to explain and defend one's exercise of it – is likely to be quite false of a number of examples of actual skills" (Annas 1995: 233; see also Annas 2001: 246). Annas's attitude toward the counterexamples is as follows:

> [The articulacy requirement] frequently meets with resistance, on the grounds that we recognize cases of expertise or skill where articulacy is not necessary (frequently gardening is proffered as an example) or where it may not seem feasible (people with physical skills are often unable to coach others who wish to acquire those skills). *Many of these cases are really cases of natural talent or of mastery of technical matters needed for exercise of the skill.*
> (Annas 2011b: 109; emphasis mine).

It seems that Annas does not think that the cases of "skill" that appear in the counterexamples are not genuine skills, for she notes that the cases "are really cases ... of mastery of technical matters needed for exercise of the skill" (quoted above). If this is the case, it might suggest that we should abandon Annas's account of expertise because such an account faces counterexamples. However, this is not the suggestion that Annas makes. What is her way out of the objection?

Here is the tactic taken by Annas:

> In any case, we have already seen that contemporary usage of the notion of skill or expertise is quite broad, and it is no surprise that it does not cover all and only the kinds of expertise that we have been looking at so far; these are

the cases that I am interested in, where we can see a sharp distinction between practical expertise and mere routine, despite some apparent shared characteristics. (Annas 2011b: 109).[19]

To explain and assess the strategy that Annas adopts to address the counterexample objection, let us consider a square of opposition about expertise: (E1) all expertise is articulate (i.e., for any skill, if a person masters the skill, then the person can articulate the general principles underlying the skill); (E2) no expertise is articulate; (E3) some expertise is articulate; (E4) some expertise is not articulate. (E1), (E2), (E3), and (E4) express four possible views about expertise. It is supposed that Annas endorses (E1), and so Stichter falsifies (E1) by providing instances of (E4). The strategy employed by Annas to respond to the counterexample objection is to make the objection misfire. Since an instance of (E4) functions as a counterexample only if there is an account of expertise that takes the form that *all* expertise is articulate, Annas clarifies her view as proposing (E3), that *some* expertise is articulate. Since at this moment there is no one who adopts the account according to which all expertise is articulate, or at least Annas does not adopt such an account, the counterexample objection misfires.

2.4 Rejoinders

Are these two strategies for defending the articulacy requirement convincing? The first strategy relies on the skill/knack distinction, which must be explained. We can take articulacy as the explanans for the distinction. But a problem arises: Is articulacy the *only* available explanans for the skill/knack distinction? Is there no other explanans that might compete with or be more promising than articulacy in explaining the distinction?

There is indeed an alternative or competing explanans. In Chapter 2, Section 7, of *The Concept of Mind* (1949), which is entitled "Intelligent Capacities versus Habits," Gilbert Ryle contrasts capacities or skills with habits.[20] According to Ryle,

---

[19] Elsewhere Annas responses in a similar manner to the counterexample objection by explaining why she is interested in a particular kind of skill: "In any case, it does not matter for this account [i.e., mastering a skill requires articulacy] if there are such cases [i.e., the cases of skill in which articulacy is not necessary], since the claim is simply that virtue has a structure which can be found in cases of skill which do exhibit the features of need for learning and drive to aspire. That we sometimes use the notion of skill more broadly than this does not affect the account" (Annas 2011a: 19).

[20] The background of this contrast is Ryle's concern with what it is that constitutes intelligent action. Assuming that an intelligent action is a manifestation of knowing-how, the question that then arises pertains to what knowing-how is. This question is discussed in Chapter 2 of *The Concept of Mind* (1949), entitled "Knowing How and Knowing That," in which Ryle proposes

> The ability to apply rules is the product of practice. It is therefore tempting to argue that competencies and skills are just habits. They are certainly second natures or acquired dispositions, but it does not follow from this that they are mere habits. Habits are one sort, but not the only sort, of second nature.
>
> (Ryle 1949: 42)

Both habits and skills are acquired dispositions, but they are not of the same sort: Habits are "simple, *single-track* dispositions, the actualizations of which are nearly uniform" (Ryle 1949: 43; emphasis mine), while skills are *multitrack* dispositions or "higher-grade dispositions ... the exercises of which are indefinitely heterogeneous" (Ryle 1949: 44). A habit can be understood as a disposition to achieve an aim in a similar situation, while a skill can be understood as a set of dispositions to achieve the same aim in a variety of situations. Here we see an alternative explanans for the skill/knack distinction: That is, what is necessary to distinguish skill from habit is multiplicity or heterogeneity.[21] This explanans is not only an alternative but also a competitor to Annas's explanans because the heterogeneous character of skill does not require an expert in a skill to articulate why he or she does what he or she does.

Now let me distinguish three sorts of dispositions:

D1: Single-track dispositions.

D2: Multitrack dispositions.

D3: Articulate (multitrack) dispositions.

Both Annas and Ryle would agree that habits (or knacks) are construed by D1. Beyond this agreement, their views about what sort of disposition suitably characterizes a skill diverge. For Ryle, skills are construed by D2 and are thus characteristically distinguished from habits. For Annas, skills are and must be construed by D3 and are thus characteristically distinguished from habits. D2 may be not only an alternative and competing explanans but also a superior one in explaining the skill/knack distinction and thus in characterizing skills. *If a skill is something the possession of which enables a subject to successfully achieve an aim in a variety of situations, then mere multitrack dispositions satisfy this condition; there is no need to ask the subject to possess an additional, articulate ability concerning the skill.* In sum, Annas's argument for the

---

two theses: The negative thesis claims that knowing-how is not a species of knowing-that, and the positive thesis claims that knowing-how is abilities, skills, or intelligent capacities. Jason Stanley and Timothy Williamson's (2001) much-discussed article "Knowing How" helps renew interest in Ryle's theses, although they challenge both theses. See Tsai 2011a, 2011b, and 2014 for a defense and elaboration of these Rylean theses.

[21] For a more detailed discussion of Ryle's distinction between skills and habits, see Tsai (2022c).

articulacy requirement is unconvincing in its current form because its second premise – that is, the claim that it is articulacy that distinguishes skill (or expertise) from knack – is open to debate due to the existence of an alternative, competing, and superior explanans.

The second strategy is also questionable. As shown in Section 2.3.2, Annas acknowledges the inarticulate "skills" that appear in the alleged counterexamples as genuine but invalidates the counterexamples by "clarifying" her claim about expertise by expressing it in the form of a particular affirmative proposition, that is, "some expertise is articulate." This clarification helps Annas not only evade the counterexamples but also to stress the point that it is the articulate kind of skill or expertise in which she is interested. However, Stichter poses a question to this kind of skill: "[I]t is not obvious why the kind of skill Annas is interested in deserves to receive the designation of 'genuine'. Our intuitive conception of skills might deserve to be thought of as genuine skills, insofar as the intellectual standards Annas discusses are counterintuitive" (Stichter 2007: 187). Recall the square of opposition about expertise in Section 2.3.2. It seems that the opponent of the articulacy requirement puts the proponent of the requirement into a predicament: When the proponent endorses (E1) ("all expertise is articulate"), the opponent falsifies this position by reference to (E4) ("some expertise is not articulate"), that is, by giving counterexamples that instantiate (E4). When the proponent, in order to deal with the counterexample objection, endorses (E3) ("some expertise is articulate"), the opponent falsifies this position by reference to (E2) ("no expertise is articulate"), that is, by highlighting the contradiction between (E2) and (E3) and by taking (E2) as intuitively correct. So, (E3) may not be intuitively correct.

The two rejoinders made in this section are at root identical: the proponent of the articulacy requirement owes us *another more convincing* argument for the thesis. The first rejoinder shows that Annas's argument from the skill/knack distinction fails to support the articulacy requirement. The second rejoinder shows that Annas's notion of articulate expertise in which she is interested may not be intuitively correct.

2.5 A New Argument for the Articulacy Requirement

I shall construct a new argument for the articulacy requirement, which I call the *argument from success-conduciveness*. I shall proceed by two steps. In the first step, I formulate a formal condition of what constitutes expertise. In the second step, I show that articulacy satisfies the formal condition stated in the first step.

2.5.1 A Formal Condition of What Constitutes Expertise

Stichter uses our intuitive conception of skills to examine Annas's account of skills. But what is it that underlies our intuitive conception of skills or expertise? Or to put it more bluntly: What is the condition of what constitutes expertise? Suppose a philosopher A claims that e_1 constitutes expertise, and another philosopher B claims that e_2 constitutes expertise. A and B can be both right or both wrong, or one right and the other wrong. To decide, we need to know what condition must be satisfied for an item to be a constituent of expertise.[22] The answer to this question would help us determine whether articulacy can be used to characterize expertise beyond merely appealing to intuitions.

Stichter indeed adopts a formal condition of what constitutes (ethical) skills, albeit only very implicitly. Let us first consider the following passage, in which Stichter criticizes the articulacy requirement:

> [B]eing virtuous is centrally a matter of *acting well*. There may be many good reasons to want a virtuous person to be able to articulate her reasons for actions in terms of general principles, but the skill analogy [of Stichter's version] rejects the idea that these intellectual requirements are necessary for acting virtuously. There are many experts in every field, while being able to *act well* within their discipline, who are not necessarily good at teaching other people this information. Demands for a greater theoretical understanding will have their source in something more than just our demand that people *act well*, since on this skill model, one can act well without having knowledge of unifying principles. (Stichter 2007: 193; emphasis mine)

Stichter seems to adopt the view that the defining feature of expertise in general is "acting well" (and, accordingly, that the defining feature of moral expertise in particular is "acting virtuously"). Let us state this view of expertise as follows: One is an expert in a certain field only if one is able to act well in that field. Stichter does not spell out what the term "acting well" actually refers to. However, it is clear that, on this view, expertise is evaluated in terms of its manifestation or performance, and further, the performance must be evaluated as "good" so that it is qualified. The term "good" (or "well") can mean many things, but Stichter's intention in this context is clear: "Good" refers mainly to being *successful* (in achieving a goal). Once one can act successfully at the behavioral level in a certain field, he or she can be regarded as an expert in that field – this view underlies what Stichter calls "our intuitive conception of

---

[22] An analogy: Some epistemologists claim that evidence constitutes knowledge, and some claim that reliability constitutes knowledge. To investigate these claims, we need a condition of what constitutes knowledge. Here, truth-conduciveness is a good candidate for this condition.

skills." Assuming that expertise is not only *success-evaluated* (in terms of assessing a manifestation of expertise) but also *success-directed* (that is, one of the fundamental aims of expertise is success), a formal condition of what constitutes expertise can be specified, roughly,[23] as follows:

(FCE) X is a constitutive element of expertise in φ only if X is *success-conducive* to achieve the goal of expertise in φ.

This condition is "formal" because it does not specify further what "X" refers to. ("X" can be substituted with *multiplicity, articulacy*, or whatever one thinks is suitable as a substitution for X.)

Given (FCE), we can explain more fully why articulacy, *from Stichter's point of view*, is not a necessary or substantive condition of expertise. Stichter thinks that, as quoted above, "Demands for a greater theoretical understanding will have their source in something more than just our demand that people act well" (Stichter 2007: 193). This thought is actually saying that articulacy, as skill in articulating the underlying and unifying principles of a particular practical skill, is *irrelevant to the success* of achieving the goal of the practical skill.

Note that articulacy is not irrelevant to any sort of success. A first-order practical skill has its own goal to achieve, and a second-order articulate skill also has its own goal to achieve, that is, the goal of articulating the underlying and unifying principles of a first-order practical skill. Thus, we can speak of both first-order success (corresponding to a first-order practical skill) and second-order success (corresponding to a second-order articulate skill). Thus construed, it is a mistake to tend to think that the problem for an articulate skill in an account of expertise lies in its being irrelevant to any sort of success. More specifically, the problem for articulacy, to put it somewhat technically, lies in its lack of *first-order* success-relevance, let alone first-order success-conduciveness. Articulacy is irrelevant to first-order success because of the observation that first-order success can be obtained without second-order success (cf. the following: "one can act well without having knowledge of unifying principles" [Stichter 2007: 193]).

So far I have, first, formulated a formal condition of what constitutes expertise (with which Stichter would agree), that is, (FCE); and, second, explained why philosophers (such as Stichter) would think that articulacy does not satisfy (FCE). The question at stake is as follows: Does articulacy *really* not satisfy (FCE)?

---

[23] This condition is rough because here I omit, among other things, considerations about an agent's *intention* and *physical condition* to use a skill.

2.5.2 Articulacy and Success-Conduciveness

Recall that Annas's argument for the articulacy requirement is based on the skill/knack distinction. Although her argument might be unsound, Annas's choice of articulacy as an explanans for the skill/knack distinction is motivated by something like (FCE). Let us examine the following passage:

> In ancient philosophy, what characterizes skill or expertise, as opposed to merely having a subrational "knack" or routine, is the ability to "give an account", where this means to explain the point of what you are doing, why you are doing this rather than that. Someone who isn't able to do this thereby reveals that he doesn't understand what he is doing (though he might, of course, still get things right if all that is required is a subrational routine). Does this answer to anything that might be found convincing in contemporary terms? If we think of how practical expertise is actually conveyed, we see at once the importance here of the giving and understanding of reasons. The apprentice builder or plumber needs to know not just *that* you lay the pipe this way, but *why*.[24] Only by being given reasons for laying the pipe this way rather than that will she be able to distinguish relevant from irrelevant factors in the situation in which she has seen the pipe laid, and only if she has a grasp of this will she **be able to lay pipe in different situations** without doing it in ways relevant to the original situation but inappropriate in the new one.
>
> (Annas 2011b: 108–109; bold emphasis mine)

For Annas, articulacy is required for expertise not only because it can be used to distinguish expertise from knack but, more importantly, articulacy exemplifies a certain feature of expertise, that is, the possession of which enables one to be able to do something (such as to lay pipes) successfully *in different types of situations*. So, a formal condition of what constitutes expertise that underlies Annas's conception of expertise is nearly the same as (FCE), which can be formulated as follows:

(FCE*) X is a constitutive element of expertise in φ only if X is success-conducive to achieve the goal of expertise in φ *in a variety of situations*.

Note that (FCE*) is not used to replace (FCE), nor is it used to modify (FCE) to integrate the situational element of expertise; such an element has already been integrated with expertise. However, (FCE*) *highlights* the situational dimension of expertise, reminding one not to forget to consider and accommodate this dimension when constructing a potential candidate for X.

Through the lens of (FCE) or its variant (which highlights a sort of situational element), one's demand for a second-order articulacy can be relevant to the

---

[24] See Little (2001) for a further elaboration of Annas's point that expertise requires knowing the "why" rather than merely knowing the "that."

demand for first-order success. Namely, when encountering certain kinds of situations, an expert's exercising a second-order articulate skill creates or enhances first-order success or avoids a first-order failure. Such situations at least include those that require a new pattern of disposition and those that require risk assessment. Let me explain these two types of situation in turn.

2.5.2.1 Situations That Require a New Pattern of Disposition

Consider the case of driving. Both a knack of driving a car and a skill in driving a car are success-conducive, but the former is success-conducive – due to its constitutive element X_1 –only in a particular type of situation (for example, only in a driving school environment, or only on the way between one's home and workplace), while the latter is success-conducive – due to its constitutive element X_2 – in a variety of types of situation (for example, in all urban road environments). X_1 might be a kind of habituality or single-track disposition-ality, while X_2 might be a kind of multiplicity or a set of multitrack dispositions. Assume that there is a driver who possesses a set of driving dispositions in which the relevant situation is limited to the urban road environment. Assume further that this driver faces a sufficiently novel situation, say, an off-road environment. If the driver now intends to become an *expert* in driving (i.e., on all road conditions and in all kinds of weather), how can his or her success in driving in an off-road environment be achieved?

The driver may try to extend his or her original set of dispositions to include a disposition to drive in an off-road environment. Such a new, first-order disposition can be acquired via a process of trial and error *from scratch* or via a process of trial and error based on the driver's second-order articulate skill. Which one is better? If the driver proceeds by trial and error from scratch, his or her success rate might be rather low. In contrast, the driver's second-order understanding of why such and such is a safe/unsafe and efficient/inefficient way of driving in an urban road environment facilitates him or her to figure out what constitutes an (un)safe and (in)efficient way of driving in an off-road environment.[25] Although the driver's second-order articulate understanding and skill is distinct from his or her (potential) first-order practical skill in driving in an off-road environment, the former is a factor that creates the latter or makes the latter possible to initiate. An articulate skill produces a kind of understand-ing-why, and such an understanding-why indicates an understanding of causes

---

[25] A single-track disposition, when extended, becomes a multitrack disposition. But it should be noted that there are two kinds of multitrack disposition (corresponding to D2 and D3 mentioned in Section 2.4). A *mere* multitrack disposition enables its possessor to obtain success in a *limited* variety of situations, while an *articulate* multitrack disposition enables its possessor to obtain success in a *greater* variety of situations.

and/or reasons that are involved in a skilled action. Grasping such causes and/or reasons enables one to (re)produce a similar skilled action in the same or different types of situations.[26]

To summarize: Consideration about the case in which an expert in a certain field faces a sufficiently novel type of situation that requires a new pattern of disposition to be created, so that the expert can achieve new and continued success in that (extended) field, shows that second-order articulacy is not so irrelevant to first-order success as originally believed.

2.5.2.2 Situations That Require Risk Assessment

Let us consider whether articulacy is required for first-order success in the *same* type of situation with which one is familiar. With regard to this question, I believe that the account of performance normativity developed by a leading virtue epistemologist, Ernest Sosa (2007, 2009, 2011, 2015), is of great help, although Sosa's main concern is epistemology.[27]

According to Sosa, a performance with an aim can be evaluated in terms of what he calls AAA structure; that is, a performance can be evaluated in terms of its *accuracy*, *adroitness*, and *aptness*. The following example illustrates Sosa's notion of the AAA structure of evaluation vividly:

> The shot aims to hit the target, and its success can be judged by whether it does so or not, by its accuracy. However accurate it may be, there is a further dimension of evaluation: namely, how skillful a shot it is, how much skill it manifests, how adroit it is. A shot might hit the bull's-eye, however, and might even manifest great skill, while failing utterly, as a shot, on a further dimension. Consider a shot diverted by a gust of wind initially, so that it would miss the target altogether but for a second gust that puts it back on track to hit the bull's-eye. This shot is both accurate and adroit, yet it is not accurate because adroit, so as to manifest the archer's skill and competence. It thus fails on a third dimension of evaluation, besides those of accuracy and adroitness: it fails to be apt. (Sosa 2011: 4)

Broadly speaking, a performance with an aim can be assessed by whether it succeeds in its aim (i.e., whether it is accurate), whether it manifests relevant competence (i.e., whether it is adroit), and whether it is accurate *because of* its adroitness (i.e., whether it is apt). The AAA structure of evaluation highlights an important aspect of skill, that is, skill must be success-conducive *in a certain way*, such as *in an apt way*.

---

[26] For a related discussion in the phenomenology of skill acquisition, see Tsai 2022b.

[27] Sosa uses this account to deal with the value problem in epistemology, that is, the problem of why knowledge is more valuable than corresponding mere true belief. Here, I do not address how Sosa applies his account to solve the value problem.

Sosa's account is not exhausted by this description, since there are two additional kinds of aptness: meta-aptness and full aptness. In some cases, a skilled operation may not be performed by an expert at a particular time because the expert in question decides not to perform it at that time due to his judgment that the operation will not succeed in that context. Here, the first-order success is not an objective, but this does not imply that the expert does nothing at all. According to Sosa, one's *forbearing* is a kind of performance with an aim, that is, avoiding (first-order) failure (Sosa 2009: 11, 2011: 6). Since forbearing is a performance, it has an AAA structure as well. That is, the performance of forbearing is meta-accurate iff it succeeds in avoiding ground-level or first-order failure; it is meta-adroit iff it manifests one's meta-competence or second-order skill in risk assessment; and third, it is meta-apt iff it is meta-accurate because of its meta-adroitness. Two notes. First, the performance of forbearing operates at the meta-level or second-order because it takes a first-order skill as its object of examination. Second, the skill corresponding to the performance of forbearing is surely located at the second-order; it is skill in risk assessment.

According to Sosa, a performance can be apt without being meta-apt, and a performance can be meta-apt without being apt (Sosa 2011: 8–9). But a performance might be both apt and meta-apt. Once this is the case, both a first-order practical skill and a second-order articulate skill[28] are exercised, and a first-order performance thus produced possesses a special property, that is, full aptness:

> A performance ... attains a special status when it is apt at the ground level while its aptness manifests competent risk assessment. Suppose this risk assessment issues in the performer's knowing that his situation (constitutional and circumstantial) is favorable (where the risk of failure is low enough) for issuing such a performance. If these conditions all obtain, then the performance's aptness might manifest its meta-aptness; thus, its aptness might be relevantly explicable as manifesting the performer's meta-knowledge that his first-order performance is likely enough to succeed and be apt. ... This applies to performances such as a shot that hits its prey. That shot is superior, more admirable and creditable, if it is not only apt, but also meta-apt, and, further, fully apt: that is, apt because meta-apt. (Sosa 2011: 9)

Sosa's notion of (full) aptness helps us see something unseen: A first-order skilled performance can be evaluated not only in terms of its success but also, and more importantly, in terms of how the success is produced. How a first-order success is produced determines the quality of the success in question.

---

[28] An articulate skill is a skill in articulating the underlying and unifying principles of a first-order practical skill. Such a skill includes telling one why such and such is *not* a way to perform an operation of a first-order skill; that is, telling one doing such and such that it will lead to failure. So, risk assessment is a part of an articulate skill.

Furthermore, a first-order success can best be entrenched within a hybrid skill system, which refers to a combination of a first-order practical skill and a second-order articulate skill.

To summarize: Consideration of the case in which an expert in a certain field faces a situation that requires a risk assessment shows that second-order articulacy can be relevant to first-order success.

Accordingly, let me formulate the argument from success-conduciveness for the articulacy requirement as follows:

(P1) Expertise is constituted by whatever it is that is (first-order) success-conducive.

(P2) Articulacy is something that is (first-order) success-conducive.

(C) Expertise is (partly) constituted by articulacy.

(P1) and (P2) are elaborated in Sections 2.5.1 and 2.5.2, respectively. I believe that this argument is more convincing than Annas's argument from the skill/knack distinction in responding to Stichter's objections. Namely, my argument discloses a formal condition of what constitutes expertise – (FCE) or (FCE*) – that is implicitly used by Stichter in constructing his account of expertise.

2.6 The Theory Extended

The issue of whether expertise requires articulacy is not a simple matter to address, or at least not as easy as first believed. I have argued that expertise requires articulacy via (FCE*). Such a view of skill or expertise is suited to the skill model of wisdom. Intuitively, we think that a wise person must give reasons for his or her actions, or that a wise person is good at advising. Without the articulacy requirement, how is it possible for a wise person to give reasons or provide advice? Given the articulacy requirement, a wise person qua an expert is required to know why he or she acts in a certain way. To put this view more formally:

> *The articulate character of wisdom qua skill*: A person S is wise only if S knows why he or she is successful at acting and living well.

This character can be incorporated into the expertise theory of wisdom *v.1*. That is, the expertise theory of wisdom *v.1* can be extended further as follows:

The Expertise Theory of Wisdom, v.2

(T1) S is wise if and only if S has skill or expertise in living well.

(T2) S is wise only if:

  (i) S knows what contributes to or constitutes well-being;

  (ii) S knows what the best means to achieve well-being are;

(iii) S is reliably successful at acting and living well (in light of what S knows); and

(iv) S knows *why* he or she is successful at acting and living well.

(T2-iv) states the articulate character of wisdom qua skill, which is supported by (T1) and the articulate character of skill. The expertise theory of wisdom *v.2* is a "skill theory" in the sense that all its conditions in (T2) are issued from the characters of skill or expertise: the goal-oriented, success-conducive, and articulate characters of skill.

3 Wisdom and Knowing What Matters

3.1 The Issue

The expertise theory of wisdom *v.2* is a partially articulated theory of wisdom. As stated in Section 1, there are several virtues of pursuing a fully articulated theory of wisdom. Aristotle also provides a fully articulated theory of wisdom, although his view of well-being is not without controversy. If the expertise theory of wisdom *v.2* can serve as a good theory of wisdom, it should be developed further into a fully articulated theory of wisdom.

3.2 Some Possible Fully Articulated Theories of Wisdom

As noted in Section 1, we can in principle construct a fully articulated theory of wisdom by combining any partially articulated theory of wisdom with any theory of well-being. The conditional (T2-i) can be specified in further detail with the assistance of hedonism, desire- satisfaction theories, or objective-list theories (let us call these three main positions on well-being "the Big Three"; see Alexandrova 2017) as follows:

(T2-i_h) S is wise only if S knows that *pleasure* contributes to or constitutes well-being.

(T2-i_d) S is wise only if S knows that *desire satisfaction* contributes to or constitutes well-being.

(T2-i_o) S is wise only if S knows that *objective goods* contribute to or constitute well-being.

Now we can have several possible fully articulated expertise theories of wisdom, such as ETW_h, ETW_d, and ETW_o.[29]

---

[29] ETW_h is composed of "(T1) S is wise if and only if S has skill or expertise in living well" and "(T2) S is wise only if (i_h) S knows that *pleasure* contributes to or constitutes well-being,

However, as said in Section 1, to be possible is one thing, while to be reasonable is another. ETW_h, ETW_d, and ETW_o can be shown to be problematic due to the widespread objections to the Big Three. A brief and general overview of these objections is as follows:

- Hedonism is wrong because things other than mental states matter.
- Desire fulfilment theories are wrong because people can desire what is bad for them.
- Objective list theories are wrong because a person may not benefit from a given good. (Alexandrova 2017: 28)

Assuming that the objections are well-grounded, ETW_h, ETW_d, and ETW_o are problematic because there are counterexamples to (T2-i$_h$), (T2-i$_d$), and (T2-i$_o$) – of the form that S is wise, but S does not *know* that such and such contributes to or constitutes well-being (S does not know, because what is "known" or believed by S regarding what it is that contributes to or constitutes well-being is wrong).[30]

If a fully articulated expertise theory of wisdom should be made not only possible but also sensible, then a true or a more defensible theory of well-being is required. Is there such a theory? In what follows, I shall introduce and develop the success theory of well-being. Before proceeding, I shall make some remarks. I do not pretend that the Big Three cannot be further modified into more sophisticated versions to overcome the objections (but there are also more sophisticated versions of the objections). Nor do I think that the success theory of well-being is the only game in town. My preference for the success theory of well-being is based on two reasons. First, the objections to the Big Three are not independent; they involve two underlying dialectical intuitions that are used to evaluate a theory of well-being. The best way for a defensible theory of well-being to deal with these intuitions is not to embrace one and reject another but rather to accommodate both. In this respect, the success theory can do the job. Second, if what we pursue is a unified theory that tells us not only what a wise person knows regarding well-being but also *how* he or she knows or deliberates about well-being, then a combination of the expertise

---

(ii) S knows what the best means to achieve well-being are, (iii) S is reliably successful at acting and living well (in light of what S knows), and (iv) S knows why he or she is successful at acting and living well." ETW_d, and ETW_o can be constructed in a similar manner.

[30] If S is wise, then S *knows* – rather than merely justifiedly believes – what constitutes well-being. For those interested in the debate between wisdom as knowledge and wisdom as rationality (or understanding), see Ryan (2013, 2016, 2017), Grimm (2015), and McCain (2020). Here, I am inclined to agree with Grimm that "what is required for wisdom is indeed *knowledge* of how to live well, as opposed to some epistemic standing short of knowledge, such as having rational (though perhaps mistaken) beliefs about how to live well" (Grimm 2015: 139).

theory of wisdom and the success theory of well-being can achieve this aim. I shall return to these two reasons in Sections 3.3 and 3.5.1, respectively.

3.3 A Better Fully Articulated Theory of Wisdom

The "success theory"[31] of well-being is introduced and developed by Simon Keller (2004, 2009), who is driven by the wish to improve the debate on well-being. In his diagnosis of the three standard theories of welfare, i.e., the mental state theory, the desire theory, and the objective-list theory (corresponding to the Big Three), Keller finds that there are two intuitions underlying the debate among various theories of well-being. These can be classified either as subjectivism (which claims, roughly speaking, that "your welfare is entirely a matter of your own attitudes" [Keller 2009: 660]) or objectivism (which claims, roughly speaking, that "we can know something about your welfare without referring to your attitudes" [Keller 2009: 660]). In opposition to the former class, anti-subjectivist intuition says that "there is no guarantee that an individual's attitudes will pick out the things that are truly in her best interests" (Keller 2009: 662). In opposition to the latter class, anti-objectivist intuition says that "your welfare – what is good *for you* – must have a very intimate connection with you; it must arise from or be grounded in facts about you" (Keller 2009: 662). To accommodate both intuitions, Keller proposes the following:

> We should try to come up with an account on which an individual's welfare is linked to the standards for success set constitutively by certain of her attitudes. If such an account could be found, it might ground the individual's welfare in his own attitudes, and hence meet anti-objectivist intuitions, but do so without identifying the individual's welfare simply with whatever happen to be the objects of his attitudes, and hence meet anti-subjectivist intuitions.
>
> (Keller 2009: 668)

The success theory emerges at this stage. One of the tasks required to implement the proposal and construct the success theory is to "identify attitudes that by nature set conditions for their own success and failure" (Keller 2009: 668). Keller identifies at least four kinds of attitudes that generate standards for their own success and failure: beliefs, goals, evaluative attitudes, and the attitude of immediately liking an experience.[32] Let us call such attitudes

---

[31] The term "success theory" is coined not by Keller himself but by Alexandrova (2017: 161). In this Element I use the term "success theory," although I prefer the term "attitude success theory" for the sake of accuracy. (In its ordinary usage, "success" might be equated with the things that most people desire, such as wealth and power. This usage might mislead some readers regarding the meaning of success in this Element. According to the success theory presented in the main text, a poor man is successful if what he desires is a fully Stoic life.)

[32] In his 2004 paper, Keller considers only one kind of attitude: goals. Bradford (2016: 798; emphasis mine) calls the view that "achievement, or something like it, is *all* there is to

"teleological attitudes" (because they all aim at something) and explain the first two kinds of attitudes in greater detail. For Keller, there are constitutive facts about beliefs and goals: beliefs aim at truth, and goals aim at achievement. Based on these facts, the standard for a belief's own success and failure is truth: A belief is successful when it is true or represents reality. The standard for a goal's success and failure is achievement: a goal is successful when it is achieved. With this explanation in hand, we can see more clearly why the success theory has the potential to meet both the anti-subjectivist and anti-objectivist intuitions. First, the success theory specifies that a person's well-being *must be* linked with his or her own (teleological) attitudes, such as his or her beliefs and goals. The anti-objectivist intuition is thus met. Second, however, there is no way to say that the person's well-being is thus simply determined by his or her own attitudes because truth (the standard for a belief's success or failure) and achievement (the standard for a goal's success or failure) are not the sort of thing that can be determined by the person's attitudes. The anti-subjectivist intuition is thus met.

Now, we can proceed to the core claim of the success theory: "An individual has a high level of welfare to the extent that she is successful, in a certain sense. To be successful in that sense is to have attitudes that do well according to the standards they constitutively set for themselves" (Keller 2009: 674). Briefly, to live well is to live successfully in a certain sense.[33] I shall say more about the success theory in Section 3.5. Here, I shall only introduce a new version of the fully articulated expertise theory of wisdom by incorporating the success theory into the expertise theory of wisdom *v.2* as follows:

The Expertise Theory of Wisdom, v.3

(T1)   S is wise if and only if S has skill or expertise in living well.

(T2)   S is wise only if

---

well-being" "achievementism" about well-being. We should note that achievementism so defined is not the same as, nor a subset of, the success theory of well-being.

[33]   As said above, Keller identifies four kinds of (teleological) attitudes that by nature set standards for their own success and failure: beliefs, goals, evaluative attitudes, and the attitude of immediately liking an experience. Unlike Keller, I add a fifth to the class of teleological attitudes: desires. Keller excludes "desires" as one of the teleological attitudes but we should note that what he says is "mere desires": "By mere desires, I mean desires that do not count as goals. I might desire a Geelong victory, but that does not mean that I take it as a goal. Mere desires, I think, do not have constitutive aims" (Keller 2009: 671). Most of what Keller says about "(mere) desires" can best be replaced by "wishes" or "hopes." Compare this with Alan Goldman's notions of desire and wish: "The primary function of desire is dispositional or motivational – desire is a state that prototypically aims to bring about its own satisfaction"; and "we ... tend to use different terms: I hope or wish for good weather, while 'I desire good weather' is somewhat unnatural" (Goldman 2018: 158).

(i$_s$) S knows that *attitude success* contributes to or constitutes well-being;

(ii) S knows what the best means to achieve well-being are;

(iii) S is reliably successful at acting and living well (in light of what S knows); and

(iv) S knows why he or she is successful at acting and living well.

The expertise theory of wisdom *v.3* is theoretically better than ETW$_h$, ETW$_d$, and ETW$_o$ because its component theory of well-being is more defensible than those associated with the Big Three in that the success theory of well-being can accommodate both the anti-subjectivist intuition and the anti-objectivist intuition, thus avoiding the counterexamples that the Big Three encounter. In the next section, I anticipate two possible objections to the expertise theory of wisdom *v.3*.

3.4 Two Challenges

3.4.1 The Objection from Bad-for-Oneself Achievements

The first objection is that the expertise theory of wisdom *v.3* is problematic because (T2-i$_s$) –that is, S is wise only if S knows that attitude success contributes to or constitutes well-being – is false. This objection goes as follows. It is possible that S is wise but does not *know* that attitude success contributes to or constitutes well-being. S does not know this because there are cases in which a person's attitude success (such as his or her belief's being true, desire's being satisfied, or goal's being achieved) does not contribute to or constitute his or her well-being. Take goal achievement as an example. It seems that there is a kind of goal achievement the possession of which is bad for the possessor's well-being, such as achievements of self-destructive or irrational goals (e.g., eating a bowl of gravel) or great achievements of the following kind: "It is hard to imagine that the wellbeing of Sir Robert Falcon Scott and his team was improved by their fateful journey to the South Pole. Yet reaching the South Pole was nonetheless a great achievement" (Bradford 2016: 795). Let us call these achievements "bad-for-oneself achievements,"[34] regardless of whether they are of the trivial type or the great type. Since the success theory is wrong due to the existence of bad-for-oneself achievements, (T2-i$_s$) is false, and, accordingly, the expertise theory of wisdom *v.3* is problematic.

3.4.2 The Objection from Evil-but-Good-for-Oneself Achievements

The second objection is that the expertise theory of wisdom *v.3* is problematic because it allows that a wise person can do evil, and it thus conflicts with

---

[34] Compare Bradford (2016), who uses the term "bad-for-you achievements."

our intuition that wisdom and evil are incompatible. In her discussion of the value of achievement, Gwen Bradford says that "there is another sense in which achievements can be bad: they can result in, say, death and destruction. Let us call these evil achievements . . . If all achievements are valuable insofar as they contribute to the wellbeing of the achiever, this entails that evil achievements benefit the achiever" (Bradford 2016: 800). Let us call evil achievements that benefit their achiever "evil-but-good-for-oneself achievements." Now, the objection to the expertise theory of wisdom *v.3* goes as follows. First, according to the expertise theory of wisdom *v.3*, a wise person S knows that attitude success contributes to or constitutes well-being. Since goal achievement is a kind of attitude success and evil-but-good-for-oneself achievements are a kind of goal achievement, S knows that evil-but-good-for-oneself achievements contribute to well-being. Second, according to the expertise theory of wisdom *v.3*, a wise person S is reliably successful at acting and living well in light of what S knows. If S indeed knows that there are particular evil achievements the possession of which contribute to his or her well-being, then S should put what he or she knows into practice rather than just knowing it. If so, it seems that the expertise theory of wisdom *v.3* allows that a wise person can do evil. Yet this conflicts with our intuition that wisdom and evil are incompatible.

3.5 The Theory Elaborated

The above two objections have something in common: They both appeal to certain kinds of attitude success to undermine the expertise theory of wisdom *v.3*. A proponent of the expertise theory of wisdom *v.3* can respond to these two objections by restricting the scope of attitude success stated in the theory. For example, the expertise theory of wisdom *v.3* can exclude bad-for-oneself achievements and evil-but-good-for-oneself achievements from its scope of attitude success. This response, however, does not delve into the nature of well-being and wisdom. The proponent of the expertise theory of wisdom *v.3* who initiates the response must tell us *exactly why* a particular kind of attitude success does not or cannot constitute well-being and wisdom, or show us the *mechanism* among attitude success, well-being, and wisdom. To achieve this, I shall address the following two issues on behalf of the proponent of the expertise theory of wisdom *v.3*. First, in what sense is a bad-for-oneself achievement "bad" for the person in question? Second, in what sense is an evil-but-good-for-oneself achievement "good" for the person in question, especially if the person is wise?

3.5.1 Wisdom and Overall Success

Assume that there is a person who has the goal of smoking ten more cigars per day and who does enjoy smoking when he smokes (Winston Churchill?). If the achievement of such a goal is "bad" for this person, why is it bad? According to the success theory of well-being proposed by Keller,

> the achievement of stupid, irrational, and self-destructive goals does indeed make a contribution to a certain aspect of welfare (it makes you more successful relative to the standards set by your own goals), but it is a contribution that is usually outweighed by its other effects, whether on that very aspect of welfare (perhaps it prevents you from achieving other, more important goals) or on others (perhaps it causes a great deal of pain).
>
> (Keller 2009: 678)

The achievement of the goal of smoking ten more cigars per day is bad for the person not because the goal *in itself* is bad but because it prevents too many other attitude success*es* that are or could be possessed by the person (say, the achievement of the goal of being healthy, which is always the basis of many other attitude successes).

Now we can see that the success theory of well-being is *self-contained* in the sense that the theory, in explaining why a bad-for-oneself achievement is bad, is not required to posit a further fundamental substance beyond attitude success; all that is required to explain one's well-being remains the idea of attitude success. Assume that a person's well-being is constituted by a dynamic set of attitude successes. A particular attitude success, actual or potential, is bad for the person's well-being if and only if this particular attitude success reduces or would reduce the set of attitude successes to a considerable extent.[35] So construed, it is *logically* possible that the goals of eating a bowl of gravel, smoking ten more cigars per day, or reaching the South Pole in a journey similar to Scott's are not bad for a person's well-being *if* the achievement of any one or all of these goals does not or cannot reduce the person's set of attitude successes to any considerable extent. However, this is *this-worldly* impossible: As human beings, our attitude successes are often related to each other in the physical, psychological, or social dimensions.

From the discussion above, we find that although *each* attitude success matters to well-being, *overall* attitude success matters more to well-being.[36]

---

[35] A person's set of attitude successes is reduced in the sense that some attitude successes in the set are removed from the set *and* returned to the person's set of attitudes. A *reduced* set of attitude successes of a person must be compared to the set of attitudes of the same person.

[36] Two notes must be made here. First, although Keller does not state that "overall attitude success matters more to well-being" explicitly, he does express a similar view: "[I]f eating gravel is a goal of such a nature that achieving it means setting back your welfare in some different respect, then that is

To incorporate this finding into our theory, the expertise theory of wisdom *v.3* can be elaborated as follows:

The Expertise Theory of Wisdom, v.4

(T1) S is wise if and only if S has skill or expertise in living well.

(T2) S is wise only if

    (i_{s*}) S knows that *overall* attitude success contributes to or constitutes well-being;

    (ii) S knows what the best means to achieve well-being are;

    (iii) S is reliably successful at acting and living well (in light of what S knows); and

    (iv) S knows why he or she is successful at acting and living well.

The mechanism among attitude success, well-being, and wisdom is now clearer. First, a person's well-being is constituted by a dynamic set of attitude successes. That is, each attitude success in the set matters to the person's well-being. Second, when a particular attitude success, actual or potential, reduces or would reduce the set of attitude successes to a considerable extent, that particular attitude success is deemed bad for the person's well-being. That is, overall attitude success matters more to the person's well-being. Third, overall attitude success does not emerge automatically; it is wisdom, I propose, that functions as an excellent evaluator, director, and mediator of attitude successes, *which do not evaluate and organize themselves*, with the aim of achieving, sustaining, and enhancing overall attitude success.

3.5.2 Wisdom and Anti-Wickedness

Let us turn to the question in what sense an evil-but-good-for-oneself achieve-ment is "good" for the person in question, especially when the person in question is a wise person.

From the point of view that each attitude success matters to well-being, it is clear that a person's evil achievement is good for the person insofar as his or her goal is achieved. However, from the point of view that overall

---

something to be said against that goal, from the point of view of your welfare; it would be better if you had a goal whose achievement is consistent with your doing well in all other respects" (Keller 2009: 678). Second, some might make the criticism that the formulation "overall attitude success matters more to well-being" (or "consistency in all respects matters more to well-being") is misleading because what *ultimately* matters remains *individual* attitude success. Indeed, in some cases, the aim of pursuing overall attitude success is to make *each* actual (or potential) attitude success as secure (or achievable) as possible. In such a case, this formulation, such a critic might suggest, should be clarified as "overall attitude success *instrumentally* matters more to well-being." However, in some cases, the aim of pursuing overall attitude success is not merely to make each attitude success secure but also to put attitude successes in a certain structure to form the "shape of a life," which matters to well-being over and above the sum of attitude successes within it. In such a case, "overall attitude success *non-instrumentally* matters more to well-being." To encompass both cases, I leave the formulation as it is; under this formulation, the function of overall attitude success remains – that is, it has the right to override a particular attitude success.

attitude success matters more to well-being, it is not yet clear whether the person's evil achievement is good for the person. A definite answer partly depends on whether the person's evil achievement reduces his or her set of attitude successes. There are two response alternatives: yes or no. If the response is the former, then the evil achievement is bad for the person. If the response is the latter, then the evil achievement is not bad (and might be good) for the person. In the second case, an evil achievement might be "doubly good" for the person (i.e., good for the person because the goal is achieved, and good for the person because the person's set of attitude successes is not reduced).

Now let us consider how a wise person would act when encountering these two alternatives. If an evil achievement is bad for the wise person, then the wise person, in order to achieve and sustain his or her overall attitude success, must prevent or remove this evil achievement from his or her set of attitude successes. If an evil achievement might be "doubly good" for the wise person, then there seems to be no reason for the wise person to prevent or remove it from his or her set of attitude successes. This possibility, in turn, seems to justify that a wise person can do evil, which is in conflict with our intuition that wisdom and evil are incompatible. Is our intuition wrong?

According to Dennis Whitcomb (2011: 103), "[m]any theorists suggest that it is impossible for wise people to be wicked," but he admits that "[t]he only argument for this view that I know of is the argument from the claim that wisdom is a virtue." The argument that Whitcomb offers, which we may call the argument from virtue, is as follows (2011: 103; my reconstruction):

1. Virtues are reliably acted on by whoever possesses them.
2. Wisdom is a virtue by which one knows how to live well.
3. Wisdom is reliably acted on by whoever possesses it so as to live well. (from 1 and 2)
4. Reliably acting so as to live well is incompatible with being wicked.
5. Wisdom is incompatible with being wicked. (from 3 and 4)

Whitcomb does not accept the argument from virtue because he argues that virtue-theoretic accounts of wisdom are mistaken. I have another reason for doubting this argument: the fourth proposition is not obviously true. Accordingly, the conclusion that wisdom is incompatible with being wicked is not persuasive, or at least requires further argumentation. So, are wisdom and evil compatible?[37]

---

[37] In one aspect, Whitcomb indeed thinks so: "The devil is evil but nonetheless wise. He was wise as an angel, and through no loss of knowledge but, rather, through some sort of affective restructuring tried and failed to take over the throne. And mere affective changes accompanied

Whitcomb constructs a new argument for the view that wisdom and evil are incompatible:

> Nonetheless, every writer about wisdom that I know of subscribes to some sort of anti-wickedness condition, at least tacitly. Furthermore, it is hard to think of actual characters in the history of literature and film, or even in our own personal lives, who are both wise and wicked. Save sinister characters like Goethe's Mephistopheles and perhaps Machiavelli, I can't think of any such characters. I conclude from these observations that if one is wise, it is unlikely that one is also evil. (Whitcomb 2011: 103)

This argument is based on unthinkability or inconceivability, which can be presented as follows: It is hard to conceive of a person who is both wise and evil (or, it is weakly conceivable that a person is both wise and evil);[38] therefore, it is improbable for a person to be both wise and evil. Let us call this the argument from weak inconceivability (hereafter, AWI).[39] Now, compare AWI with the argument from strong inconceivability (hereafter, ASI), which can be presented as follows: It is strongly inconceivable that a person is both wise and evil; therefore, it is impossible for a person to be both wise and evil. Both arguments aim to show that wisdom and evil are incompatible but with different ranges of applicability (i.e., being applicable merely to the actual world or to all possible worlds). The second, ASI, leaves no room for the possibility of being both wise and evil, whereas the first, AWI, makes room for this possibility, though remote. Regarding these two arguments, I side with AWI rather than ASI due to argumentative considerations. If valid, ASI must assume that inconceivability implies impossibility, which, in turn, assumes that we can conceive of every possibility; in contrast, AWI has no such *controversial* assumptions. Directed by this comparison, AWI is less vulnerable to criticism, and its conclusion can be enhanced by emphasizing its character as follows: It is improbable, but not impossible, for a wise person to do evil.

In addition to the argument from virtue and the argument from inconceivability (either ASI or AWI), there is a third related[40] argument associated with

---

by no loss of knowledge should not remove one's wisdom. So, wisdom and evil are compatible" (Whitcomb 2011: 103).

[38] Below is a list of nominations for wise persons: Ghandi, Confucius, Jesus Christ, M. L. King, Socrates, Mother Theresa, Solomon, Buddha, the Pope, Oprah Winfrey, Winston Churchill, the Dali Lama, Ann Landers, Nelson Mandela, and Queen Elizabeth II (cf. Paulhus et al. 2002: 1053). Can these individuals be conceived of as evil persons?

[39] My usage of the terms "strong inconceivability" and "weak inconceivability," here and later, conforms roughly to that of Tim Bayne, who suggests that "[a] scenario is strongly inconceivable for S when S seems to see that it is impossible, whereas a scenario is weakly inconceivable for S when S cannot see that it is possible" (Bayne 2010: 43). That S cannot see that it is possible does not entail that S seems to see that it is impossible.

[40] I use the word "related" because some might argue that "wisdom is good" is not identical to "wisdom is anti-wicked."

wisdom and its correlative; call it the argument from definition: "Wisdom could not fall short of The Good because if it did, it would not be wisdom. Saying that wisdom is good would then be like saying that a triangle is three-sided. Nothing could show that a triangle is not three-sided, nor that wisdom is not good" (Kekes 2020: 59). That is, the view that wisdom is good is true *by definition*. (By the same token, one can argue that wisdom is anti-wicked because this is true *by definition*.) The argument from definition, however, is not persuasive. We still wonder what the reason is for choosing one particular definition rather than another. As Kekes says, "This would not be a *reason* for thinking that wisdom is good but a stipulative definition . . . that ignores the question of what makes the connection between wisdom and The Good necessary" (Kekes 2020: 59; emphasis in the original).

Based on the above, the objection from evil-but-good-for-oneself achievement can be defused. The kernel of this objection is the intuition that wisdom and evil are necessarily incompatible. This intuition, however, is ungrounded (if not groundless) because the arguments for it (such as the argument from virtue, ASI, and the argument from definition) have been shown to be problematic for a variety of reasons. What is left is AWI. However, strictly speaking, AWI does not support the intuition and accordingly does not reject the expertise theory of wisdom constructed in the previous sections (either the expertise theory of wisdom *v.3* or *v.4*). In fact, both AWI and the expertise theory of wisdom *v.4* make room for the possibility, though very remote, of being both wise and evil.

My explanation of the relationship between wisdom and evil is as follows. As I have argued, a wise person can do evil when the evil achievement is doubly good for the wise person; that is, it is possible for a wise person to do evil. However, I suggest that this is a logical possibility rather than an actual possibility because, as Whitcomb observes, there is no such exemplar in the actual world. But why is there no actual exemplar of a person who is both wise and evil? An explanation, or hypothesis, for the observed phenomenon that all wise persons in our actual world are anti-wicked is, I suggest, that *all evil achievements are bad for the well-being of practically wise persons in our actual world*. Recall that if an evil achievement is bad for a wise person, then in order to achieve and sustain his overall attitude success, the wise person must prevent or remove this evil achievement from his set of attitude successes. Briefly, if an evil achievement is bad for the wise person's overall attitude success, the wise person qua wise must be anti-wicked.

But how is it possible that all evil achievements are bad for the well-being of practically wise persons in our actual world? This is possible if all practically wise persons in our actual world have a special set of attitude successes that could be easily reduced to a considerable extent by an evil achievement.

For example, and in particular, if a wise person has an attitude of *promoting others' well-being* within his set of attitude successes,[41] and if the achievement of the very attitude has an integrated relationship with other attitude successes within the set, then such an integrated set is sensitive to and can be considerably reduced by an evil achievement, which is generally understood as an achievement of *harming the well-being of other people*.

I have completed my responses to the two objections raised in Section 3.4. As can be seen, these objections help elaborate rather than undermine the expertise theory of wisdom *v.4*.

3.6 The Expertise Theory of Wisdom: Its Base and Extension

Let me conclude this section with two remarks, one regarding the philosophy of wisdom and another regarding the psychology of wisdom.

First, the underlying concern of this Element is the nature of wisdom, and the underlying questions are fundamental and familiar: What is wisdom? What does a practically wise person know? To fully address these questions in the philosophy of wisdom, I have developed and argued for a fully articulated theory of wisdom by integrating the expertise theory of wisdom with the success theory of well-being. According to the expertise theory of wisdom *v.4*, a person is wise if and only if he or she has skill or expertise in living well, which is constituted by his or her knowing that overall attitude success constitutes well-being, knowing what the best means to achieve well-being are, and being successful at acting and living well in light of what he or she knows. The expertise theory of wisdom *v.4* is structural in that it has two supplements: the Base and the Extension. The Base of the expertise theory of wisdom *v.4*, or the metatheory of the expertise theory of wisdom *v.4*, consists of the General Argument, the goal-oriented, success-conducive, and articulate characters of wisdom qua skill and the others-caring feature of wisdom. The Base of the expertise theory of wisdom *v.4* can explain certain platitudes about wisdom, such as that a wise person must think about the ends and the means, must put what he or she knows about well-being into practice, and must be anti-wicked. The Extension of the expertise theory of wisdom *v.4* (most of which is stated in Section 3.5) is about the *mechanism* among attitude success, well-being, and wisdom, which can be summarized as follows: (a) well-being is constituted by a dynamic set of attitude successes; (b) the set of attitude successes can be enhanced or reduced (relative to the set of attitudes); (c) each attitude success

---

[41] Promoting others' well-being does not entail sacrificing one's well-being or overall attitude successes. Following Zagzebski (2017), we can distinguish sages (whom we admire for their acts of wisdom) from saints (whom we admire for their acts of self-sacrifice).

matters to the set of attitude successes; (d) overall attitude success matters more to the set of attitude successes; (e) certain attitude successes can reduce the set of attitude successes to a considerable extent; (f) wisdom is the good evaluator, director, and mediator of attitude successes to achieve, sustain, and enhance overall attitude success; and (g) all practically wise persons in our actual world have a certain kind of set of attitude successes that could easily be reduced to a considerable extent by an evil achievement.

Note: The four versions of the expertise theory of wisdom can be seen as four stages of the development of a substantive expertise theory of wisdom. The first version shows the basic idea of the expertise theory. The second version shows that the idea of skill or expertise in the expertise theory is hybrid skill. The third and four versions are about the notion of well-being in the expertise theory. In Part III, I shall use the capitalized term "Expertise Theory of Wisdom" to refer to the expertise theory of wisdom *v.4* unless otherwise noted.

Part III   The Theory Defended

4 The Deliberation Objection: Deliberation about Final Ends

4.1 The Issue

The objections to the skill model of wisdom can be applied to the Expertise Theory of Wisdom. We can classify these objections into two types. The first type argues that certain distinct features are present in wisdom but not in skill and concludes that wisdom cannot be modeled by skill. The second type argues that certain distinct features are present in skill but not in wisdom and concludes that wisdom is not skill. A special case of the first type of objection is that a person with practical wisdom should deliberate about the (final) end being pursued, but a person with a practical skill cannot be required to do so (cf. Hacker-Wright 2015 and Stichter 2018; see Tsai 2020 for discussion).[42] Let us call this case the Deliberation Objection. A special case of the second type of objection is that practical skill has sufficient feedback for learning and improvement, but practical wisdom has no such feedback. Let us call this case the Feedback Objection. In this section, I consider whether the Expertise Theory of Wisdom in particular, and the skill model of wisdom in general, can rebut the Deliberation Objection.

John Hacker-Wright (2015: 983) has argued that "the claimed identity does not exist and . . . the analogy is liable to lead us to overlook what is distinctive about

---

[42] Another case of the first type of objection is that a wise person has the motivation to do what he knows, whereas an expert in a certain domain is not required to have motivation to do what he knows how to do. See Swartwood (2013: 525–6) and Stichter (2018).

practical wisdom." The reason to which Hacker-Wright appeals is that an essential component of wisdom cannot be accounted for either by the Identity Thesis or the Analogy Thesis, that is, "having a *correct* conception of worthwhile end or ends" (Hacker-Wright 2015: 983; emphasis mine). However, advocates of the skill model might not overlook the value component of wisdom completely; they may simply believe that the value component must be addressed outside the skill model. For example, according to Annas (2011a: 100), "There is an important point about virtue which is not illuminated by the skill analogy ... It emerges when we reflect that we admire people who have virtues, find them inspiring, and take them as ideals." For Annas (2011a: 105), "what makes virtue admirable and inspiring as an ideal" lies in its "commitment to goodness." Annas notes the role of the "commitment to goodness" in the practical reasoning of a virtuous person but believes that this value component is not, and cannot be, illuminated by the skill model. Matt Stichter, another major advocate of the skill model, also claims that "there is [an] important feature of virtue that may not be so easily captured on the skill model"; that is, "virtues are said to require practical wisdom, where practical wisdom concerns what is good and what is bad for human beings" (Stichter 2016: 443), whereas "[s]kills involve knowing how to achieve the end of the skill, but this doesn't involve making value judgments about the end being pursued ... which is part of *phronesis*" (Stichter 2016: 446).

Although advocates of the skill model do not overlook the value component of wisdom, both advocates and opponents of the skill model are convinced that the model is limited in its explanatory power. Advocates caution us about – and opponents criticize – this limitation. What underlies the criticism and caution to the skill model involves functional asymmetries between wisdom and skill: A person with wisdom *can* and *should* deliberate about the end being pursued (accordingly and consequently, wisdom is constituted by, e.g., a correct conception of a worthwhile life [Hacker-Wright], a lifelong commitment to goodness [Annas], or a correct value judgment about what a good life is [Stichter]). By contrast, a person with a particular skill cannot deliberate about the end that the skill is being used to pursue, and even if he or she can, he or she is not required to do so. Are these asymmetries real?

4.2 The Asymmetry Argument A

As a representative opponent of the skill model, Hacker-Wright argues against versions of the skill model (such as the Identity Thesis and the Analogy Thesis) as follows:

> [T]here is a component of practical wisdom that creates a crucial distinction between practical wisdom and skill in that it requires a correct conception of

worthwhile ends. This component of practical wisdom requires a virtuous agent to undertake a distinctive sort of reflection not required for possessing skill. To achieve practical wisdom ... we must engage in reflection on our life considered as a whole, and develop a view of what it is to live well that includes deciding which activities are worth pursuing. (Hacker-Wright 2015: 984)

Hacker-Wright sees a functional asymmetry between wisdom and skill, which can be described as follows:

(W_1) A person with practical wisdom *should* deliberate about the (overarching) end of practical wisdom.

(S_1) A person with a practical skill *is not required to* deliberate about the (overarching) end of the practical skill.

For Hacker-Wright, the above asymmetry has its origin in a more fundamental asymmetry between wisdom and skill. To illustrate this origin, we will examine the received view of practical deliberation or reasoning that is best characterized by Elijah Millgram as follows:

The received view in this area [i.e., area of practical reasoning] is instrumentalism, which has it that all practical reasoning is means–end reasoning. That is, it holds that practical reasoning consists in finding ways to attain one's goals or ends ... Instrumentalism is an exclusionary position; since it holds that *only* means–end reasoning counts as practical reasoning, there is no such thing as reasoning about what one's ultimate or primary or final ends ... should be in the first place. (Millgram 2008: 732)

According to the instrumentalist view of practical deliberation:

(In1) All practical deliberation is means–end deliberation; and

(In2) Means–end deliberation can only be about a means to an end rather than an (overarching) end in itself.[43]

Hacker-Wright attributes this instrumentalist view, particularly its (In2), to deliberation that constitutes a practical skill.[44] Thus, a further and fundamental functional asymmetry arises between practical wisdom and practical skill:

(W_2) A person with practical wisdom *can* deliberate about the (overarching) end of practical wisdom.

---

[43] An instrumentalist can take (In1) without accepting (In2); see, for example, David Schmidtz (1994), who introduces the notion of *maieutic end* and explains how final ends can be rationally chosen through this notion.

[44] Compare Hacker-Wright (2015: 984–985). Several other relevant passages in this regard can be found in the same article.

(S_2) A person with a practical skill *cannot* deliberate about the (overarching) end of the practical skill.

Now we can reconstruct Hacker-Wright's objection to the skill model in general, and to Swartwood's expert skill model in particular, in the form of an argument:

(P_1) All the distinctive features of wisdom can be explained by the features of skill (by the skill model).

(P_2) A person with wisdom *can* and *should* deliberate about the end of wisdom (by W_1 and W_2).

(P_3) A person with a skill *cannot* or *is not required to* deliberate about the end of the skill (by S_1 and S_2).

(C_1) Thus, there are distinctive features of wisdom that are not features of skill (by P_2 and P_3).

(C_2) Thus, it is not the case that all the distinctive features of wisdom can be explained by the features of skill (by P_1 and C_1).

Call this the *Asymmetry Argument A*. The argument, however, is unsound, and the problematic lies in (P_3). In Sections 4.3 and 4.4, I argue for the (compound) thesis that a person with a practical skill *can* and *should* deliberate about the end of the skill.

4.3 Why an Expert Can Deliberate about Final Ends

Similarly to Hacker-Wright, Stichter (although he is a vocal advocate of the skill model) believes that "skills are properly classified as mere expressions of instrumental rationality, while practical wisdom requires value rationality – not just selecting the correct means, but reasoning correctly about what ends to follow" (Stichter 2016: 445). Why can't an expert in a practical skill deliberate about the end of the skill? According to Stichter (2016: 446), "[w]ith skills, the end being pursued is essentially fixed – in chess, it's winning the game." This explanation echoes what Aristotle said in the *Nicomachean Ethics*:[45]

> We deliberate not about ends but about means. For a doctor does not deliber-
> ate whether he shall heal, nor an orator whether he shall convince, nor
> a statesman whether he shall produce law and order, nor does any one else

---

[45] Although there is still a debate about whether Aristotle is an instrumentalist regarding practical deliberation, I will not address that matter in this Element. For those who are interested in this debate, see Kolnai (1962) and Wiggins (1975–1976).

deliberate about his end. Having set the end, they consider how and by what means it is to be attained. (Aristotle 2009: Book III, 1112b10–15)

Chess masters, doctors, orators, and statesmen are persons with certain particular practical skills: chess skills, medical skills, public speech skills, and governmental skills, respectively. The ends of these skills are fixed: winning chess games, healing people with illness, convincing people to believe or do something, and producing law and order in society. A criterion implicitly adopted by Stichter is that if an end is fixed, the end cannot be the subject of deliberation. However, this criterion becomes problematic when the case of practical wisdom is taken into consideration. Let us first consider whether the end of practical wisdom is fixed. For Stichter, the answer is negative because when comparing practical skill and practical wisdom, he believes that "practical wisdom requires value rationality – not just selecting the correct means, but reasoning correctly about what ends to follow" (Stichter 2016: 445). However, in this construal, has the end of practical wisdom, which requires value rationality, not been fixed by the things that are valuable in human life? The overarching end of practical wisdom is essentially or constitutively fixed by *well-being* (or living well, or living a good life). Although well-being can be construed as different things – such as happiness, flourishing, pleasure, life-satisfaction, and so forth – all these things are valuable in human life. Assuming that the end of practical wisdom is fixed, if the end of a particular practical skill cannot be the subject of deliberation because it is fixed, then neither can the end of practical wisdom because it too is fixed.

However, Stichter believes that the end of practical wisdom can be the subject of deliberation. If the end of practical wisdom (which is fixed) can be the subject of deliberation, so too can the overarching end of a practical skill (which is also fixed). At this juncture, we can learn something from considering how the end of practical wisdom can be the subject of deliberation. One suggestion begins with the observation that the end of practical wisdom, although fixed, is nonetheless vaguely specified. When we say that well-being can be happiness, flourishing, pleasure, or life-satisfaction, what we are saying is that well-being can be *specified* as happiness, flourishing, pleasure, or life-satisfaction. These are not things to replace well-being but are precisely the candidate specifications of well-being. Against this background one can deliberate which specification characterizes well-being best.[46] Thus, to put it more generally, one can deliberate about fixed ends because one can deliberate about or choose among various specifications of the overarching ends. The above suggestion is inspired by specificationism about practical deliberation, according to which

---

[46] I explain what the term "best" means in Section 4.5.

"[d]eliberation consists ... not, or not only, in determining what would be a means to one's already given ends, but in coming to understand what would constitute realizing a vaguely specified end" (Millgram 1997: 135). The rationale for favoring specificationism over instrumentalism, as Millgram puts it, is as follows: "Since many of our ends are simply too vague or indefinite to serve as starting points for means–end reasoning, instrumentalist practical reasoning could not get going if one did not first further specify the overly indefinite ends" (Millgram 2008: 732).[47]

The specificationist account of practical deliberation lends support to the thesis that an expert in a particular practical skill can deliberate about the end of the skill. Thus, as implied by this thesis, a doctor can deliberate about the end of the medical skill that he or she possesses, that is, healing people with illness (for example, he or she can deliberate whether euthanasia, understood as the termination of life by a doctor at the request of a patient, is part of healing people with illness); an orator can deliberate about the end of the public speech skill that he or she possesses, that is, convincing people to believe or do things; and a statesman can deliberate about the end of the governing skill that he or she possesses, that is, producing a good constitution. However, some might object by saying that the specificationist account of deliberation only applies to the kind of deliberation whose end is vaguely/broadly specified or unspecified, whereas the ends of practical skills, such as those in the Olympics, are not of this kind – the ends of skills in the Olympics must be precisely specified so that athletes' performances can be measured objectively.

With regard to this kind of objection, I have three responses. First, when critics try to undermine my thesis by arguing that the ends of practical skills are not vaguely specified, they should make explicit the quantifiers over the domain of practical skills. If what the critics claim is that the ends of *all* practical skills are not vaguely specified, then the claim is very probably false. If what they claim is that the ends of *some* practical skills are not vaguely specified, the claim does not deny that experts *in some domains* can deliberate about the ends of the skills they possess.

Second, even if the ends of some practical skills are precisely specified, caution should be paid to whether such precisely specified ends are the result of deliberation. And, if so, then merely offering examples of skills with precisely specified ends does not prove that the end of a skill cannot be the subject of deliberation. Consider, for instance, swimming skill. Its fixed but broadly

---

[47] For Millgram, specificationism and instrumentalism are two distinct positions, but for Tiberius (2000), specificationism is simply a kind of instrumentalism. The present Element will not address this matter. For a book-length development of specificationism, see Richardson (1994).

specified end (say, having mobility and feeling comfortable in aquatic environments) can be further specified in diverse ways based on how swimming's role is construed: The end of swimming-as-competition would be very different from the end of swimming-as-physical-therapy or the end of swimming-as-survival (because time and distance matter in swimming-as-competition but might not in swimming-as-physical-therapy and swimming-as-survival).[48] Assuming that the end of the swimming skill is not broadly specified (e.g., the precisely specified ends in the Olympics), such a precisely specified end is nonetheless actually a particular end-specification – rather than a replacement – for the fixed but broadly specified end of swimming skill (if it were a replacement, then swimming-as-physical-therapy and swimming-as-survival would no longer be treated as swimming).[49] Thus, some cases in which the end of a practical skill is precisely specified prove, rather than disprove, that the end of the skill is the subject of deliberation.

Third, even when the end of a practical skill is precisely specified, the specified end can still be the subject of deliberation as a result of expert skill development, because – here I follow Barbara Montero, who in turn follows Anders Ericsson – expertise requires deliberate practice, which requires setting new ends or goals that exceed one's current level of performance. Thus, Montero (2016: 64) defines expertise as follows: "experts are individuals who have engaged in around ten or more years of deliberate practice, which means close to daily, extended practice with the specific aim of improving, and are still intent on improving." She further spells out the notion of deliberate practice:

> Deliberate practice ... according to Ericsson, prevents the attainment of automaticity and allows for ongoing improvement. "The key challenge for aspiring expert performers," he tells us, "is to avoid the arrested development associated with automaticity," and the way to accomplish this is by "actively setting new goals and higher performance standards, which require them to increase speed, accuracy, and control over their actions" (Ericsson 2008: 991).

---

[48] Like the debates about well-being at the theoretical-construction level (for some, pleasure matters most, while for others, it does not), no theoretical consensus has been reached on what swimming is (for some, distance matters most, while for others it does not). Compare the following: "Currently, there is no universally accepted definition of swimming ability ... [S]wimming ability is frequently evaluated in terms of distance swum, stroke used and time taken. With respect to drowning prevention, this definition is problematic" (Brenner et al. 2006: 112–113). I am not suggesting that incompatibility of end-specifications is a feature of skill but that such an incompatibility *can* occur in both wisdom and skills (and thus that there is no asymmetry between wisdom and skills in this respect).

[49] In other words, the reason why the fixed but vaguely/broadly specified end of a skill φ cannot be replaced by a further specified end is that the former end plays the role of circumscribing the scope of the skill φ in a variety of forms. The fixed but vaguely/broadly specified end of the skill φ not only determines whether a particular skill belongs to the category of the skill φ but also constitutes the most general feature of skills within this category.

> Because deliberate practice aims to achieve goals just beyond one's reach, it
> precludes complete automaticity. (Montero 2016: 129)

Although Montero aims to argue for the idea that expertise precludes complete automaticity due to deliberate practice, her rationale, that expertise requires deliberate practice, suits the purpose of this Element: It shows that the precisely specified end of an expert skill can be revised so as to advance the skill to a higher level. For example, a swimmer can respecify his or her end or goal of swimming from a previously specified end, say, swimming 100 meters in 1 minute, to a newly specified end, say, swimming 100 meters in 55 seconds, which exceeds his or her current level of performance. Thus, an expert with a particular practical skill can deliberate about the end of the skill regardless of whether the end is specified vaguely or precisely.

4.4 Why an Expert Should Deliberate about Final Ends

Even if a person *can* deliberate about the end, it does not imply that the person *should* deliberate about the end. To complete my argument against the Asymmetry Argument A, a further argument is needed for the thesis that an expert with a practical skill should deliberate about the end. To make this argument, I consider a question that has not yet been mentioned but that must not be overlooked: What is it that makes a constitutive element of a practical skill *constitutive*? For example, in Section 1, we saw that in the expert skill model, the five subskills are treated as the constitutive elements of an expert decision-making skill. Why are these five subskills, but not others, treated as constituent elements of an expert decision-making skill? We can answer this question by noting that these subskills reliably contribute, directly or indirectly, to success in *making accurate decisions*, which is the end of an expert decision-making skill. In this light, I suggest that the reason why these subskills are the constitutive elements of an expert decision-making skill in a particular domain is that they are conducive to the success of achieving the end of the expert decision-making skill in that domain.

So construed, a deliberative skill is success-conducive. Let us now turn to the question of what a deliberative skill that constitutes a particular practical skill, such as swimming, does in achieving the end of the practical skill. One answer is that the deliberative skill is exercised to choose the most effective means to achieve the end. However, is this all that the deliberative skill can do? The answer to this question is negative because of the success-conduciveness of the deliberative skill. An agent's deliberative skill is also exercised to choose or construct the *best* specification for the fixed but vaguely/broadly specified end – where "best" means that the end, under a particular specification, is the most realistically, reproducibly, and/or challengingly achievable end for the agent in question. Consider the swimming skill we addressed in Section 4.3. Its fixed but broadly specified end is having mobility and feeling comfortable in aquatic environments. A novice might specify the vaguely specified end further as swimming 100 meters freestyle in 50 seconds; this end, however, is unrealistic for a novice. In this case, the specification is not good for the agent in question because of the consideration of skill acquisition. A competent swimmer might specify the broadly specified end further as swimming 100 meters freestyle in 5 minutes; this end, although realistically and reproducibly achievable, is not challenging for a competent swimmer. In this case, the specification is not best for the agent in question because of the consideration of skill improvement. An athlete might specify the broadly specified end further as swimming 100 meters freestyle in 45 seconds with doping; this end, although realistically and challengingly achievable, is difficult to achieve reproducibly over a span of several years (due to the adverse health consequences of doping). In this case, the specification is not best for the agent in question because of the consideration of long-term success in competition.

If a deliberative skill that constitutes a particular practical skill is success-conducive, as addressed above, any factor highly relevant to the success of achieving the end of the practical skill should be taken as the subject of deliberation. In this respect, the specification of an end is highly relevant to success as well as the means to an end. If one should deliberate about a means to an end because the effectiveness of the means is highly relevant or contributes to the success of achieving the end, then one should also deliberate about the end of the practical skill because the specification of the end is highly relevant or contributes to the success of achieving the end. The examples from the previous paragraph show that a further specification of the fixed but broadly specified end of swimming is relevant to the success of achieving the end – success in realizing ends at different levels, such as initial skill acquisition, skill improvement, and skill retention over the long term.

Thus far, I have argued that a person with a practical skill not only *can* but also *should* deliberate about the end of the skill. Thus, the Asymmetry Argument A is unsound, and the Deliberation Objection is rebutted.

4.5 Deliberation in The Expertise Theory of Wisdom

What I would like to say more is about how a wise person, understood by the Expertise Theory of Wisdom, deliberates about final ends.

Because the Species Thesis considers practical wisdom as a species of practical skill, there must be a specific difference between practical wisdom and its cognate species. What is this specific difference? Let us consider a possible answer that Stichter offers. Stichter illustrates three cases that demonstrate that practical wisdom (*phronesis*) and practical skill are distinct from one another:

> CHESS. With skills, the end being pursued is essentially fixed – in chess, it's winning the game. Skills involve knowing how to achieve the end of the skill, but this doesn't involve making value judgments about the end being pursued (say, about the worth of playing chess) – which is part of *phronesis*.
>
> (Stichter 2016: 446; heading added)

> TENNIS. [O]n the way to a tennis match the expert tennis player comes across the scene of an automobile accident, and . . . she decides to help the accident victims . . . This involves her making a value judgment about the relative worth of playing tennis versus saving lives . . . and so draws on *phronesis*. Presumably, though, we wouldn't think that this makes her any better qua tennis player; and so that element of *phronesis* is not part of being an expert performer. (Stichter 2016: 446; heading added)

> TORTURE. [T]here seem to be skills that on the whole are morally vicious, like torture. One could become an expert at torturing, and remain responsive to the distinctive demands of the practice, without having *phronesis*.
>
> (Stichter 2016: 446; heading added)

I agree with Stichter that *phronesis* and skills are distinct, but I disagree with him that the distinction lies in that the former involves making value judgments about the end being pursued, whereas the latter does not. Stichter's rationale for the distinction is that an expert in a skill *cannot* deliberate about the end of the skill, but this rationale has been critically examined and undermined in Section 4.3. In the version of the skill model that I favor, being able to make (prudential) value judgments is not the specific difference between practical wisdom and its cognate species; on the contrary, it is an attribute possessed by all practical skills, including practical wisdom. If the specific difference between practical wisdom and its cognate species does not lie in the making of value judgments, where does it lie? The answer is that it is the broadest specification of the end of practical wisdom: well-being or living well. More generally, in my account of skill, the broadest specification of the end of a particular skill (say, having mobility in aquatic environments as the broadest specification of the end of swimming skill), which circumscribes the scope of the skill in a variety of forms (say, freestyle stroke, breaststroke, and jellyfish float), constitutes the most general but nevertheless essential feature of the skill in question. Farming, building, navigating, golfing, driving, swimming, and *phronesis* are all species of the same genus, that is, practical skill, but they are distinguished from one another by their ends specified in the broadest sense.

I conclude this section with three cases of practical skills that shed light on how similar (yet unique) practical wisdom is compared to other practical skills.

PHRONESIS. In the skill model that I propose, a person with practical wisdom, like an expert in a practical skill, can and should deliberate about the end of practical wisdom, that is, well-being or living well. The deliberative skill that constitutes practical wisdom, call it D_W,[50] is exercised to choose or construct the best specification for living well (as one of its main functions) – "best" in the sense that the chosen or constructed specification is the most realistically, reproducibly, and/or challengingly achievable specification *for the agent in question*. So construed, different agents can have different "equally best" specifications of well-being, such as living sensually, living pleasurably, living virtuously, and so on.[51]

CHESS*. In my general account of skill, a person with chess skill *can* and *should* deliberate about the (fixed but vaguely specified) end of chess skill, that is, winning chess games. (Cf. CHESS, in which the end is fixed and cannot be deliberated about.) The deliberative skill that constitutes chess skill, call it D_C, is exercised to choose or construct the best specification for winning chess games (as one of its main functions). There are several possible specifications for winning chess games, such as winning games fairly/unfairly, or winning games over Deep Blue/human chess masters/ordinary chess players. (Training processes would be quite different depending on which specification is chosen or constructed.) In light of the abovementioned criterion for "best" – for an ordinary chess player – winning unfairly might not be the best specification because such an end, typically speaking, cannot be reproducibly achievable. Winning over Deep Blue (or a computer program such as AlphaGo) is not the best specification either because such an end is unrealistic.

TORTURE*. Similarly, in my account of skill, a person with torture skill can and should deliberate about the fixed but broadly specified end of torturing, that is, intentionally causing severe pain or suffering. The deliberative skill that constitutes torture skill, call it D_T, is exercised to choose or construct the best specification for intentionally causing severe pain or suffering (as one of its main functions). There are several possible specifications for causing severe

---

[50] A deliberative skill that constitutes a particular practical skill, such as D_W, is domain-specific, as one might be good at deliberating about living well but bad at deliberating about, say, winning chess games, and vice versa.

[51] Recall that my theory of wisdom can yield an account of well-being that is compatible with Simon Keller's achievementist view of well-being, according to which, first, "[a]n individual's achieving her goals *in itself* contributes to her welfare *regardless* of what those goals are" (Keller 2004: 28), and second, "the greater the effort required for an individual to achieve her goal, the more her welfare is enhanced by its achievement" (Keller 2004: 34; see Keller 2009 for development and defense of this view; see Bradford 2016 and Bradford and Keller 2016 for discussion).

pain or suffering, such as causing severe *physical* pain or suffering, or causing severe *mental* pain or suffering. In TORTURE, Stichter distinguishes torture skill from *phronesis* by (positive) moral appraisal – *phronesis* is morally virtuous, whereas torture skill is morally vicious. However, it is not necessarily so. *Phronesis*, as addressed in PHRONESIS, can be morally neutral. And, for some, "torture might . . . in extreme emergencies be morally justified" (Miller 2017). If *phronesis* is not a *moral* subset of practical skills, then Stichter requires another explanation of how various practical skills, *phronesis* included, are distinguished.

5 The Feedback Objection: Feedback for Skill Acquisition

5.1 The Issue

In this section we consider whether the skill model of wisdom in general and the Expertise Theory of Wisdom in particular can rebut the Feedback Objection mentioned in Section 4, the core of which states that wisdom is not skill because skill requires sufficient feedback for learning and improvement, but wisdom does not have such feedback.

It seems to be commonsensical that sufficient feedback is a condition for learning and improving a skill. However, forming and receiving sufficient feedback has its own conditions that must be met. According to Daniel Kahneman and Gary Klein, "a regular environment and an adequate opportunity to learn" are "preconditions for the development of skills, including intuitive skills" (Kahneman and Klein 2009: 520). That is, they argue that two conditions must be satisfied for the development of skill and skilled intuition. The first necessary condition is an environment of sufficient *regularity* or sufficiently *high validity* – "the environment must provide adequately valid cues to the nature of the situation" (Kahneman and Klein 2009: 520). The second necessary condition is an adequate *opportunity to learn*, that is, "people must have an opportunity to learn the relevant cues [or the regularities of that environment]" (Kahneman and Klein 2009: 520). The first condition is more fundamental than the second since the latter is possible only if the former is satisfied.

The notion of "validity" is used to describe "the causal and statistical structure of the relevant environment" (Kahneman and Klein 2009: 520). The validity of a task environment is determined by the relationships between cues and the outcomes of possible actions. If the relationship between those factors is stable or regular, then the validity is high; otherwise, it is low. If a high-validity environment is necessary for developing skill and expert intuition, then it seems that a "skill" is impossible in some fields or professions due to their low-validity environments:

We describe task environments as "high-validity" if there are stable relationships between objectively identifiable cues and subsequent events or between cues and the outcomes of possible actions. Medicine and firefighting are practiced in environments of fairly high validity. In contrast, outcomes are effectively unpredictable in zero-validity environments. To a good approximation, predictions of the future value of individual stocks and long-term forecasts of political events are made in a zero-validity environment.

(Kahneman and Klein 2009: 524).

Let us return to our main concern and ask: In what kind of environments, high-validity or low-validity, is wisdom practiced? If wisdom is practiced in low-validity environments, how can it receive adequate feedback? And if wisdom has no adequate (let alone sufficient) feedback for learning and improvement, how can it be treated as skill or expertise?

5.2 The Asymmetry Argument B

Daniel Jacobson (2005) poses an objection to the skill model of wisdom. Swartwood expresses this objection as follows:

Jacobson (2005) identifies another pressing objection for the expert skill model. Since the expert skill model shows that wisdom can be developed only if a person gets sufficient feedback on the quality of her decisions, developing wisdom is possible only if a person can get sufficient feedback on the quality of her all things-considered decisions about what to do. But, Jacobson argues, no such feedback is available. While it is clear how we can get feedback on how our chess moves contribute to winning, it is much less clear how any of the (often objectionably parochial) sources of feedback we get on the wisdom of our decisions could help us develop a highly reliable understanding of what to do. If Jacobson is right, then wisdom is not "a plausible human skill" after all. (Swartwood 2013: 527)

This objection can be formulated in the form of an argument as follows:

(P1) All expert skills require sufficient feedback for learning and improvement.

(P2) Wisdom does not have adequate, let alone sufficient, feedback for learning and improvement.

(C) Thus, wisdom is not expert skill.

Let us call this argument the *Asymmetry Argument B*.

In the following sections, I will show that the argument is not as sound as it appears to be because both of its premises are disputable (if not obviously false). In Section 5.3, I examine (P1) by considering whether all skills require sufficient feedback for learning and improvement. In Section 5.4, I examine (P2) by discussing whether wisdom does not have adequate feedback for learning and improvement. In Section 5.5, I consider how the Expertise Theory of Wisdom can respond to the Feedback Objection based on what is stated in Sections 5.3 and 5.4.

5.3 Do All Expert Skills Require Sufficient Feedback for Learning and Improvement?

To address the question presented in the heading above, I begin by discussing naturalistic decision-making (NDM).[52] NDM is concerned with "how people actually make decisions in real-world settings" (Klein 2008: 456). Note that NDM focuses on a particular kind of people and a particular kind of real-world situation. First, NDM focuses on "the *experts who perform a constant task* (e.g., putting out fires; establishing a diagnosis) but encounter unfamiliar situations" (Kahneman and Klein 2009: 522; emphasis mine). Second, NDM is fascinated with "*ill-structured, uncertain, dynamic, ill-defined environments* with multiple event-feedback loops, multiple players, and organizational norms and goals that must be balanced against the decision makers' personal choice" (Schraagen 2018: 491; emphasis mine). Putting together the two points, NDM is concerned with expertise in low-validity environments. Against this background, Jan Schraagen finds that NDM's fascination with ill-structured environments

> makes one wonder *how true expertise can ever be acquired in such environ-ments*. If environments are truly characterized by the factors listed above [i.e., ill-structured, uncertain, dynamic, ill-defined, etc.], they are surely more representative of low-validity environments such as the stock market or the political arena than of high-validity environments. Consequently, such nat-uralistic environments are unconducive, to say the least, of becoming an expert. (Schraagen 2018: 491; emphasis mine)

Although skill and expertise require high-validity environments, Schraagen thinks that skill and expertise are possible in naturalistic environments, which are "more representative of low-validity environments." But how is this pos-sible? Schraagen argues that

> it would be too hasty to conclude that genuine expertise does not exist in naturalistic environments. All we may conclude is that we will mostly encounter, as analysts, isolated islands of knowledge in seas of ignorance – in other words, humans with bounded rationality. And we may predict that when experts in a particular area of expertise are confronted with problems

---

[52] Compare: "The word 'naturalistic' in NDM . . . refers to real-world situations, as contrasted with laboratory situations, rather than 'natural situations' in the sense of 'taking place in nature'" (Schraagen 2018: 487).

that are entirely new to them, they may be able to use some of their knowledge, for instance a general approach to solving problems in their domain,
but they will display more novice-like behavior the more novel the problems
become. (Schraagen 2018: 491)

What Schraagen suggests is not that a novice can become an expert in a skill
domain by learning in low-validity environments. On the contrary, the
novice still needs high-validity environments and an opportunity to learn
the relevant cues of the environments. What he suggests is that experts are
not all-knowing because there are unknown situations in their skill domain;
however, experts are more knowledgeable, experienced, and skilled than
others in coping with novel situations and low-validity environments in their
skill domain.

Gary Klein, a leading NDM researcher, raises the idea of "fractionated
expertise," according to which "professionals exhibited genuine expertise in
some of their activities but not in others" (Kahneman and Klein 2009: 522). He
thinks that

> [t]here are a few activities, such as chess, in which a master will not encounter
> challenges that are genuinely new. In most domains, however, professionals
> will occasionally have to deal with situations and tasks that they have not had
> an opportunity to master. Physicians, as is well known, encounter from time
> to time diagnostic problems that are entirely new to them – they have
> expertise in some diagnoses but not in others.
>
> (Kahneman and Klein 2009: 522)

However, can physicians not develop expertise to cope with novel or low-
validity environments? For Klein,

> *[t]he ability to recognize that a situation is anomalous and poses a novel
> challenge is one of the manifestations of authentic expertise*. Descriptions of
> diagnostic thinking in medicine emphasize the intuitive ability of some
> physicians to realize that the characteristics of a case do not fit into any
> familiar category and call for a deliberate search for the true diagnosis.
>
> (Kahneman and Klein 2009: 522–523; emphasis mine)

Klein does not conclude from the idea of fractionated expertise that expertise is
impossible in low-validity environments.

NDM research helps us see things in a bigger picture. Most skill domains
involve both high-validity and low-validity environments. Professionals can
exhibit their skillfulness in both high-validity and low-validity environments.
Professionals' skillfulness in high-validity environments can be treated as
fractionated expertise, and their skillfulness in low-validity environments can
be treated as "adaptive expertise." It is clear that the possibility of skillfulness in

low-validity or naturalistic environments does not presuppose that there exists sufficient feedback in such environments.

How is it possible for experts to develop (adaptive) expertise in novel, low-validity, or naturalistic environments in their skill domains? In my view, there is no standard operating procedure in this context, but authentic experts *know how to navigate* in such environments. For example, as mentioned above, Klein thinks that authentic experts are able to recognize that a situation is anomalous and poses a novel problem. Schraagen thinks that authentic experts are able to use some of their knowledge, such as "a general approach to solving problems in their domain," to solve novel problems, although "they will display more novice-like behavior the more novel the problems become" (Schraagen 2018: 491).

Schraagen's idea echoes that expressed by Hubert Dreyfus and Stuart Dreyfus. In *Mind over Machine*, Dreyfus and Dreyfus propose a five-stage model of skill acquisition according to which an individual learning a skill progresses through five stages: novice, advanced beginner, competence, proficiency, and expertise. Intuition is the hallmark of expertise: "*When things are proceeding normally, experts don't solve problems and don't make decisions; they do what normally works*" (Dreyfus and Dreyfus 1986: 30–31; italics in original). That said, Dreyfusians also point out,

> Even for experts, novel situations may still be encountered (in some skill domains more than others). . . . If the situation is sufficiently novel or atypical and no intuitive perspective is available or obvious, or if more than one intuitive perspective suggests itself, the expert may fall back on deliberating about which perspective to adopt or to paying attention to situational aspects which call for the application of situational maxims.
>
> (Rousse and Dreyfus 2021: 20)[53]

Accordingly, the first premise of the Asymmetry Argument B, that is, (P1) "All expert skills require sufficient feedback for learning and improvement,"

---

[53] In their later writings (Dreyfus 2001, 2017, Dreyfus and Dreyfus 2008, Rousse and Dreyfus 2021), Dreyfus and Dreyfus add a sixth stage: *Mastery*. For them, deliberation does not occur at the level of expertise but only at the levels either below or above it. When an expert is situated outside the range of normal conditions, he or she either has no developed intuitions or, if he or she does have such intuitions, they require further examination. According to Dreyfus and Dreyfus, rationality or deliberation exercised below the level of expertise is called "calculative rationality" or "calculative deliberation": "In calculative deliberation, the performer, lacking an intuitive perspective on the situation, reverts to general rules or situational maxims for guidance on how to proceed" (Rousse and Dreyfus 2021: 22). Furthermore, rationality or deliberation exercised above the level of expertise is called "deliberative rationality" or "perspectival deliberation": "In perspectival deliberation, the expert performer already perceives the situation in light of an intuitive perspective that occurs to her on the basis of past experience. . . . [H]ere the deliberation involves testing limits, imagining alternatives, or seeking to improve the intuitive perspective that has occurred to the performer" (Rousse and Dreyfus 2021: 22).

is disputable. This premise is either false or true but misleading. The premise is false if adaptive expertise is possible. The premise is true if the term "expert skills" in the premise refers to fractionated expertise, but it is misleading because it assumes that authentic expertise is nothing but fractionated expertise or that authentic expertise has nothing to do with novel or low-validity environments in its skill domain. These assumptions are questionable. Recall that "[t]here are a few activities, such as chess, in which a master will not encounter challenges that are genuinely new" (Kahneman and Klein 2009: 522). It seems to be conceivable and plausible that most, if not all, expertise skills, as a form of authentic expertise, require the person who possesses them to be able to cope with both high-validity and low-validity environments in their skill domain. The idea of fractionated expertise serves as an expediency rather than the whole truth. If (P1) is disputable, then the Asymmetry Argument B is not as sound as it appears to be.

5.4 Does Wisdom Not Have Adequate Feedback for Learning and Improvement?

Let us turn to (P2) of the Asymmetry Argument B. Some philosophers think that wisdom does not have adequate, let alone sufficient, feedback for learning and improvement. Let us consider and examine two reasons for this thought.

5.4.1 The Goal of Wisdom Is Too Broad or Vague

The first reason is that wisdom does not have a clear-cut end or goal and thus cannot have adequate feedback. According to Matt Stichter,

> [T]here is a further problem with conceptualizing wisdom as the singular skill of getting it right in the moral domain. This runs into the problem that skills require feedback for improvement, and so there needs to be some identifiable goal to the exercise of your skill ... It might be argued that virtue has an identifiable fixed goal like other skill domains, which would be *eudaimonia* (or living well). However, it is difficult to see how the feedback mechanism would work if wisdom is a skill in the sense of a singular all-things-considered judgment about how to act well morally. The specific problem is that the target of living well in that sense is very broad and vague, which will make it difficult to determine whether you are acting in such a way as to achieve success. (Stichter 2018: 133)

Assume that a good all-things-considered judgment about how to live well is the final end or goal of wisdom. The conception of well-being embedded in this goal is broad and vague. Does this imply that wisdom cannot receive adequate feedback and therefore is not a skill? This inference might be too hasty. One of the reasons is that the conception of well-being has not yet been precisely specified.

Skills are goal-oriented. But the goal of a skill is not understood in a one-dimensional way. The goal of a skill can be specified either very precisely or by category. When the goal of a skill is specified by (superordinate) category, it is usually specified in a very broad or vague manner. A broadly/vaguely specified goal, by its nature, makes it difficult to determine whether it has been achieved, but such a goal shows the most general and essential feature of the skill with that goal. For example, the goal of a doctor's skill is making people healthy or healing people with illness. This goal-specification is broad or vague, but it defines the essence of the doctor's skill. A doctor with this broadly/vaguely specified goal of medical skill can be in a better position to think about questions such as whether and how a doctor can assist patients in terminating their lives on request. (Cf: How does or can a doctor with only a very precisely specified goal of medical skill deliberate about the issue of euthanasia?) What has been said above, however, does not imply that a broadly/vaguely specified goal of a skill cannot be further specified in a more precise manner.

Likewise, the goal of wisdom qua skill can be specified either broadly or precisely. This goal can be specified broadly as "living a good life" (cf. Kekes 1983) or as "achieving a common good" (cf. Sternberg 1998). These broad goal-specifications can be specified in further detail. For example, "living a good life" can be specified more precisely as "living a good life in terms of fulfilling one's own values, or in terms of satisfying one's own desires." "Achieving a common good" can be specified more precisely as "achieving a common good through a balance among intrapersonal, interpersonal, and extrapersonal interests" (cf. Sternberg 1998). Obviously, these more precise goal-specifications can be specified further.

In sum, the broadness/vagueness of the goal of a skill (and wisdom) does not preclude the precision of the goal of the skill (and wisdom). Thus, the idea that the goal of wisdom is broad or vague does not imply that wisdom cannot receive *adequate* feedback and is therefore not a skill. That said, we should note that we are not saying that wisdom must have *sufficient* feedback. However, even if wisdom does not always get sufficient feedback, this does not imply that wisdom is not a skill. This leads us back to the issue, discussed in Section 5.3, of whether all expert skills require sufficient feedback for learning and improvement. If wisdom is authentic expertise, it must be able to be exercised in both high-validity and low-validity environments. And in low-validity environments, by their very nature, sufficient feedback is difficult.

5.4.2 Feedback for Wisdom Is Contentious

The second reason for the idea that wisdom does not have adequate feedback for learning and improvement is that feedback for wisdom is contentious. Let us consider Jacobson's objection to the skill model of wisdom:

> Such a robust conception of practical wisdom seems to be the sine qua non of moral knowledge. The trouble is that the ability described is not a plausible human skill. Recall that the skill model depends crucially on the identification of non-contentious success conditions and the availability of feedback. Without feedback from success and failure, practice at an activity will not tend to make one any better at it. Habituation into virtue works because emotional rewards and sanctions gradually alter a person's affective responses and motivational tendencies, in ways that can correct them. Yet people regret decisions that turn out badly according to their own criteria and triumph in success judged by their own lights – not to concordance with some independent "space of reasons." Granted, some forms of feedback can arise from other sources, most notably the culture in which we live. Shame and guilt in response to the contempt or anger of others, for instance, along with pride in response to positive social recognition, help condition our responses so as to accord better with the expectations of peers and authorities. But social feedback cannot inculcate such robust practical wisdom either, since the socially accepted consideration may not be the truly salient one.
>
> (Jacobson 2005: 400)

Jacobson does not explicitly say that the goal of wisdom is too broad to formulate feedback on goal achievement. What he says is that various forms of feedback for learning and improving wisdom are contentious. What kinds of feedback are examined by Jacobson? One kind is (what we may call) personal feedback, such as feedback from one's own criteria or standards, and the other kind is social feedback, such as the contempt and anger of others. Why are these forms of feedback contentious? It seems that for Jacobson, personal feedback may be unjustifiably subjective, and social feedback may be groundlessly conventional. (Or, to use Swartwood's terminology, such feedback is "often objectionably parochial" [Swartwood 2013: 527].) Since all these kinds of feedback for learning and improving wisdom can be cast into doubt for a variety of reasons, wisdom, Jacobson concludes, "is not a plausible human skill."

To respond to this objection, let us consider the concept of feedback in motor skill acquisition. In motor learning and control, feedback can be classified into two major categories: intrinsic (or inherent) feedback and extrinsic (or augmented) feedback. Intrinsic feedback is information the performer directly receives from his or her sensory systems during a performance. Such information can be divided into two forms: proprioceptive feedback, which comes from sources within a person's body, and exteroceptive feedback, which comes from sources outside a person's body (cf. Schmidt and Wrisberg 2008: 285). For example, an archer can "feel" the position of his or her limbs as well as the muscles in his or her upper back and shoulder blades working when he or she draws a bow. The archer can also "see" the arrow hitting (or missing) the target. Extrinsic feedback is "information that is provided to the learner by some outside source, such as the comments of an instructor or therapist, the digital display of a stopwatch, the displayed scored of a gymnastics judge, the film of a game, the videotape replay of a movement" (Schmidt and Wrisberg 2008: 286).

The importance of feedback in learning a motor skill is that such feedback can improve or correct one's performance. But how does this process work? Consider first whether a person receiving sensory feedback that "the arrow does not hit the board" implies that the person receives sensory feedback that "the arrow *misses the target*." I think not. The latter adds something more to the sensory feedback. What is it that is added?

> In many situations, *inherent feedback* requires almost no evaluation at all; one sees that the bat missed the ball or one can feel the fall while walking on an icy sidewalk. Thus, some errors seem to be signaled immediately and clearly. But other aspects of inherent feedback are not so easily understood, and perhaps the performer must *learn* to recognize their occurrence and evaluate what the feedback means. Examples might be the gymnast learning to sense whether or not the knees are bent during a movement, or a patient with a recent hip replacement who is learning to put partial weight through the leg while walking with canes. It is thought that inherent feedback is compared to a learned **reference of correctness**, with this reference acting in conjunction with the feedback in an error-detection process. Without such a reference of correctness, many forms of inherent feedback probably cannot be used to detect errors. (Schmidt et al. 2019: 342; bold emphasis mine)

Feedback can be corrective only if it is in conjunction with a *reference of correction*. According to Schmidt et al., "a *reference of correctness* is generated that will serve as the standard against which the feedback from the performance is judged. . . . We can think of this reference as a representation of the feedback qualities associated with moving as planned or as intended" (Schmidt et al. 2019: 151). The way in which the conjunction of feedback and a reference of correctness operates within a system (human or machine) can be expressed as follows:

> Then, via the reference of correctness, the system can compare the feedback it receives with the feedback it expects to receive. If feedback from the two sources is the same, the implication is that the movement is correct and that no

adjustments are necessary. But if a difference exists between the feedback received and the reference, then an error is signaled and a correction is required. (Schmidt et al. 2019: 151)

Sensory feedback "the arrow misses the target" appears to be descriptive, but it is actually an evaluative judgment.

Now we can have a clearer understanding of why or in what sense feedback for wisdom that Jacobson examines is contentious. The reason is *not* because feedback for wisdom is "personal" or "social" – they are merely classifications of the *sources* of feedback. The reason lies in the reference of correctness, which is tied in with feedback for wisdom. If personal feedback for wisdom is unjustifiably subjective, this is not because such feedback is "personal" but rather because the reference of correctness tied in with it is unjustifiably subjective. If social feedback for wisdom is groundlessly conventional, this is not because the feedback is "social" but rather because the reference of correctness tied in with it is groundlessly conventional.

The most important reference of correctness tied in with feedback for wisdom is concerned with the goal of wisdom (i.e., well-being). A learner of a skill needs feedback for him or her to know whether he or she has achieved the goal of the skill. So, if wisdom is a skill, a learner of wisdom needs feedback regarding goal achievement. But what is the content of a reference of *goal-correctness* tied in with feedback for wisdom? If the content is a person's personal opinion of well-being, then the reference may be subjective. If the content is a society's myths about well-being, then the reference may be groundless. However, what if the content is a person's or a society's *rationally justified or justifiable* conception of well-being? For example, hedonistic, desire-satisfaction, and objective-list conceptions of well-being are all qualified candidates (although I prefer the attitude-success conception of well-being; see Section 5.5 for a brief explanation of this point). All these conceptions are more defensible than conceptions of well-being that are based merely on personal opinions and social conventions. Via a rationally justified or justifiable reference of goal-correctness, a learner of wisdom can compare the feedback that he or she receives with the feedback that he or she expects to receive and thus gets corrective feedback for wisdom. Such corrective feedback for wisdom is noncontentious to a certain extent, or at least, it is not "objectionably parochial" (Swartwood 2013: 527).

So far, I have argued that we can defuse the Feedback Objection by undermining the argument for it: Both premises of the Asymmetry Argument B are not as solid as they appear to be. In sum, wisdom can have adequate corrective feedback for learning and improvement if the goal of wisdom can be specified, and if what is thus specified is rationally justifiable rather than vulnerable.

5.5 Feedback in The Expertise Theory of Wisdom

The Expertise Theory of Wisdom constructed and developed in this Element is a *fully articulated* theory of wisdom, and the conception of well-being embedded in it is *rationally defensible*. In this way, and to a certain extent, the Expertise Theory of Wisdom can be made invulnerable to the Feedback Objection.

For the Expertise Theory of Wisdom, the goal of wisdom, that is, well-being or living well, is first and foremost specified in terms of overall attitude success, and wisdom is understood in terms of something the possession of which enables one to achieve, sustain, and enhance overall attitude success. Corrective feedback for learning wisdom, as argued above, must tie in with a reference of correctness. For the Expertise Theory of Wisdom, the reference of goal-correctness tied in with feedback for wisdom is overall attitude success. That is, the feedback that a learner of wisdom expects to receive is that his or her attitude successes are overall achieved, sustained, or enhanced. Here is a toy example. Assume that a person S has fulfilled goals G1–G5 and pursued goals G6–G10. (G1 to G10 might be structured hierarchically; that is, some are means-goals, and some are end-goals.) Now, if S has a new desire to smoke two packs of cigarettes per day and decides to fulfill this desire, S receives negative feedback if G1–G10 (or the core goal in the goal hierarchy) must take good health as a precondition. The corrective feedback that S receives might be expressed as "the satisfaction of the desire to smoke two packs of cigarettes per day undermines G1–G5 and blocks G6–G10."

This discussion is merely a sketch. The contents of one's teleological attitudes must be specified and made specific, and the relations among attitudes should be structured hierarchically. I leave this task to the readers. For the Expertise Theory of Wisdom, the specific contents of teleological attitudes vary from person to person. So, the specific way to achieve, sustain, and enhance one's overall attitude success varies from person to person (although there might be patterns, as specific agents with specific attitudes can be considered as a *kind* of agent). Seen from this perspective, wisdom learning and training, like good athletic training, is tailor-made for each individual. Receiving feedback for learning and improving wisdom requires a deeply personal endeavor.

Conclusion

There are many different *notions* of wisdom in the literature and across different cultures,[54] but not all of these notions have been developed into *theories* that explain wisdom in a systematic way. Readers can understand the aim of this Element as the demonstration of how far a skill model of wisdom (or a skill-based notion of wisdom) can go with respect to explaining various aspects of wisdom.

The skill model of wisdom developed and defended in this Element explains several crucial aspects of wisdom. Section 1 explains the nature of wisdom: Wisdom is a species of skill. Section 2 explains the structure of wisdom: Wisdom is bi-leveled. Section 3 explains the content of wisdom: A wise agent knows that overall attitude success matters most. Section 4 explains the norms involved in wisdom: A wise agent pursues the final goal whose specification is the most realistically, reproducibly, and/or challengingly achievable for the agent in question. Section 5 explains the acquisition of wisdom: Wisdom is acquired via feedback which is tied in with the rationally justified/justifiable references of correctness.

---

[54] For example, see Curnow (2015), in which he explores various notions of wisdom from historical perspectives, and Yang and Intezari (2019), who provide an overview of laypeople's conceptions of wisdom in non-Western cultures.

Appendix: The Expertise Theory of Wisdom, Four Versions

(Words in italics indicate the main differences from the previous version of the theory.)

The Expertise Theory of Wisdom, v.1
(T1) S is wise if and only if S has skill or expertise in living well.

(T2) S is wise only if
- (i) S knows what contributes to or constitutes well-being;
- (ii) S knows what the best means to achieve well-being are; and
- (iii) S is reliably successful at acting and living well (in light of what S knows).

The Expertise Theory of Wisdom, v.2
(T1) S is wise if and only if S has skill or expertise in living well.

(T2) S is wise only if
- (i) S knows what contributes to or constitutes well-being;
- (ii) S knows what the best means to achieve well-being are;
- (iii) S is reliably successful at acting and living well (in light of what S knows); and
- (iv) *S knows why he or she is successful at acting and living well.*

The Expertise Theory of Wisdom, v.3
(T1) S is wise if and only if S has skill or expertise in living well.

(T2) S is wise only if
- (i$_s$) S knows that *attitude success* contributes to or constitutes well-being;
- (ii) S knows what the best means to achieve well-being are;
- (iii) S is reliably successful at acting and living well (in light of what S knows); and
- (iv) S knows why he or she is successful at acting and living well.

The Expertise Theory of Wisdom, v.4
(T1) S is wise if and only if S has skill or expertise in living well.

(T2) S is wise only if

(i$_{s*}$) S knows that *overall* attitude success contributes to or constitutes well-being;

(ii) S knows what the best means to achieve well-being are;

(iii) S is reliably successful at acting and living well (in light of what S knows); and

(iv) S knows why he or she is successful at acting and living well.

References

Alexandrova, A. (2017). *A Philosophy for the Science of Well-Being* (Oxford: Oxford University Press).

Angier, T. (2010). *Techne in Aristotle's Ethics: Crafting the Moral Life* (London: Continuum).

Annas, J. (1993). *The Morality of Happiness* (Oxford: Oxford University Press).

Annas, J. (1995). "Virtue as a Skill," *International Journal of Philosophical Studies* 2(2): 227–243.

Annas, J. (2001). "Moral Knowledge as Practical Knowledge," *Social Philosophy and Policy* 18: 236–256.

Annas, J. (2003). "The Structure of Virtue," in M. DePaul and L. Zagzebski (eds.), *Intellectual Virtue: Perspectives from Ethics and Epistemology* (Oxford: Oxford University Press), pp. 15–33.

Annas, J. (2008). "The Phenomenology of Virtue," *Phenomenology and the Cognitive Sciences* 7: 21–34.

Annas, J. (2011a). *Intelligent Virtue* (Oxford: Oxford University Press).

Annas, J. (2011b). "Practical Expertise," in J. Bengson and M. A. Moffett (eds.), *Knowing How: Essays on Knowledge, Mind, and Action* (Oxford: Oxford University Press), pp. 101–112.

Aristotle (2009). *The Nicomachean Ethics* (trans. D. Ross) (Oxford: Oxford University Press).

Baehr, J. (2012). "Two Types of Wisdom," *Acta Analytica* 27(2): 81–97.

Baltes, P. and Staudinger, U. (2000). "Wisdom: A Metaheuristic (Pragmatic) to Orchestrate Mind and Virtue toward Excellence," *American Psychologist* 55: 122–136.

Bayne, T. (2010). *The Unity of Consciousness* (Oxford: Oxford University Press).

Bengson, J. and Moffett, M. (2011). "Two Conceptions of Mind and Action," in J. Bengson and M. Moffett (eds.), *Knowing How: Essays on Knowledge, Mind, and Action* (Oxford: Oxford University Press), pp. 3–55.

Benner, P. (2001). *From Novice to Expert: Excellence and Power in Clinical Nursing Practice* (Commemorative Edition) (Upper Saddle River, NJ: Prentice Hall).

Bloomfield, P. (2000). "Virtue Epistemology and the Epistemology of Virtue," *Philosophy and Phenomenological Research* 60(1): 23–43.

Bloomfield, P. (2001). *Moral Reality* (Oxford: Oxford University Press).

Bloomfield, P. (2014). *The Virtues of Happiness: A Theory of the Good Life* (Oxford: Oxford University Press).

Bluck, S. and Glück, J. (2005). "From the Inside Out: People's Implicit Theories of Wisdom," in R. Sternberg and J. Jordan (eds.), *A Handbook of Wisdom: Psychological Perspectives* (Cambridge: Cambridge University Press), pp. 84–109.

Bradford, G. (2016). "Achievement, Well-Being, and Value," *Philosophy Compass* 11: 795–803.

Bradford, G. and Keller, S. (2016). "Well-Being and Achievement," in G. Fletcher (ed.), *The Routledge Handbook of Philosophy of Well-Being* (New York: Routledge), pp. 271–280.

Brenner, R., Moran, K., Stallman, R., Gilchrist, J., and McVan, J. (2006). "Swimming Abilities, Water Safety Education and Drowning Prevention," in J. Bierens (ed.), *Handbook on Drowning: Prevention, Rescue, Treatment* (Berlin: Springer), pp. 112–116.

Curnow, T. (2015). *Wisdom: A History* (London: Reaktion Books).

Dreyfus, H. (2001). *On the Internet* (London: Routledge).

Dreyfus, H. (2017). "On Expertise and Embodiment: Insights from Maurice Merleau-Ponty and Samuel Todes," in J. Sandberg, L. Rouleau, A. Langley, and H. Tsoukas (eds.), *Skillful Performance: Enacting Capabilities, Knowledge, Competence, and Expertise in Organizations* (Oxford: Oxford University Press), pp. 147–159.

Dreyfus, H. and Dreyfus, S. (1986). *Mind over Machine: The Power of Human Intuition and Expertise in the Era of the Computer* (Oxford: Blackwell).

Dreyfus, H. and Dreyfus, S. (1991). "Towards a Phenomenology of Ethical Expertise," *Human Studies* 14(4): 229–250.

Dreyfus H. and Dreyfus, S. (2008). "Beyond Expertise: Some Preliminary Thoughts on Mastery," in K. Nielsen, S. Brinkmann, C. Elmholdt, et al. (eds.), *A Qualitative Stance: Essays in Honor of Steiner Kvale* (Aarhus: Aarhus University Press), pp. 113–124.

Ericsson, K. (2008). "Deliberate Practice and Acquisition of Expert Performance: A General Overview," *Academic Emergency Medicine* 15(11): 988–994.

Ericsson, K., Charness, N., Feltovich, P., and Hoffman, R. (eds.) (2006). *The Cambridge Handbook of Expertise and Expert Performance* (Cambridge: Cambridge University Press).

Ferrari, M. and Kim, J. (2019). "Educating for Wisdom," in R. Sternberg and J. Glück (eds.), *The Cambridge Handbook of Wisdom* (Cambridge: Cambridge University Press), pp. 347–371.

Goldman, A. (2018). *Life's Values: Pleasure, Happiness, Well-Being, and Meaning* (Oxford: Oxford University Press).

Grimm, S. (2015). "Wisdom," *Australasian Journal of Philosophy* 93: 139–154.

Hacker-Wright, J. (2015). "Skill, Practical Wisdom, and Ethical Naturalism," *Ethical Theory and Moral Practice* 18(5): 983–993.

Hetherington, S. (2011). *How to Know: A Practicalist Conception of Knowledge* (Malden, MA: Wiley–Blackwell).

Hetherington, S. (2021). "Knowledge as Skill," in E. Fridland and C. Pavese (eds.), *The Routledge Handbook of Philosophy of Skill and Expertise* (New York: Routledge), pp. 168–178.

Hursthouse, R. (2006). "Practical Wisdom: A Mundane Account," *Proceedings of the Aristotelian Society* 106: 285–309.

Jacobson, D. (2005). "Seeing by Feeling: Virtues, Skills, and Moral Perception," *Ethical Theory and Moral Practice* 8: 387–409.

Kahneman, D. and Klein, G. (2009). "Conditions for Intuitive Expertise: A Failure to Disagree," *American Psychologist* 64(6): 515–526.

Kekes, J. (1983). "Wisdom," *American Philosophical Quarterly* 20(3): 277–286.

Kekes, J. (2020). *Wisdom: A Humanistic Conception* (Oxford: Oxford University Press).

Keller, S. (2004). "Welfare and the Achievement of Goals," *Philosophical Studies* 121: 27–41.

Keller, S. (2009). "Welfare as Success," *Nous* 43: 656–683.

Klein, G. A. (2008). "Naturalistic Decision-Making," *Human Factors* 50(3): 456–460.

Kolnai, A. (1962). "Deliberation Is of Ends," *Proceedings of the Aristotelian Society* 62(1): 195–218.

Little, M. O. (2001). "On Knowing the 'Why': Particularism and Moral Theory," *Hastings Center Report* 31(4): 32–40.

McCain, K. (2020). "What the Debasing Demon Teaches Us about Wisdom," *Acta Analytica* 35: 521–530.

Miller, S. (2017). "Torture," *The Stanford Encyclopedia of Philosophy* (Summer 2017 Edition), ed. E. N. Zalta, https://plato.stanford.edu/archives/sum2017/entries/torture/.

Millgram, E. (1997). *Practical Induction* (Cambridge, MA: Harvard University Press).

Millgram, E. (2008). "Specificationism," in J. E. Adler and L. J. Rips (eds.), *Reasoning: Studies of Human Inference and Its Foundations* (Cambridge: Cambridge University Press), pp. 731–747.

Montero, B. (2016). *Thought in Action: Expertise and the Conscious Mind* (Oxford: Oxford University Press).

Nightingale, A. W. (2004). *Spectacles of Truth in Classical Greek Philosophy* (Cambridge: Cambridge University Press).

Nozick, R. (1989). "What Is Wisdom and Why Do Philosophers Love It So?," in R. Nozick, *The Examined Life* (New York: Touchstone Press), pp. 267–278.

Paulhus, D., Wher, P., Harms, P., and Strasser, D. (2002). "Use of Exemplar Surveys to Reveal Implicit Types of Intelligence," *Personality and Social Psychology Bulletin* 28: 1051–1062.

Richardson, H. (1994). *Practical Reasoning about Final Ends* (Cambridge: Cambridge University Press).

Rousse, B. and Dreyfus, S. (2021). "Revisiting the Six Stages of Skill Acquisition," in E. Mangiante and K. Peno (eds.), *Teaching and Learning for Adult Skill Acquisition: Applying the Dreyfus & Dreyfus Model in Different Fields* (Charlotte, NC: Information Age Publishing), pp. 3–28.

Russell, D. (2009). *Practical Intelligence and the Virtues* (Oxford: Oxford University Press).

Russell, D. (2012). *Happiness for Humans* (Oxford: Oxford University Press).

Ryan, S. (2013). "Wisdom," *The Stanford Encyclopedia of Philosophy* (Winter 2014 Edition), ed. E. N. Zalta, http://plato.stanford.edu/archives/win2014/entries/wisdom/.

Ryan, S. (2016). "Wisdom: Understanding and the Good Life," *Acta Analytica* 31: 235–251.

Ryan, S. (2017). "A Deeper Defense of the Deep Rationality Theory of Wisdom," *Acta Analytica* 32: 115–123.

Ryle, G. (1949). *The Concept of Mind* (Chicago, IL: University of Chicago Press; new edition, 2000).

Schmidt, R. and Wrisberg, C. (2008). *Motor Learning and Performance: A Situation-Based Learning Approach*, 4th edition (Champaign, IL: Human Kinetics).

Schmidt, R., Lee, T., Winstein, C., Wulf, G., and Zelaznik, H. N. (2019). *Motor Control and Learning: A Behavioral Emphasis*, 6th edition (Champaign, IL: Human Kinetics).

Schmidtz, D. (1994). "Choosing Ends," *Ethics* 104(2): 226–251.

Schraagen, J. (2018). "Naturalistic Decision Making," in L. J. Ball and V. A. Thompson (eds.), *The Routledge International Handbook of Thinking and Reasoning* (London: Routledge), pp. 487–501.

Sosa, E. (2007). *A Virtue Epistemology: Apt Belief and Reflective Knowledge*, Vol. 1 (Oxford: Oxford University Press).

Sosa, E. (2009). "Knowing Full Well: The Normativity of Beliefs as Performances," *Philosophical Studies* 142: 5–15.

Sosa, E. (2011). *Knowing Full Well* (Princeton, NJ: Princeton University Press).

Sosa, E. (2015). *Judgment and Agency* (Oxford: Oxford University Press).

Stalnaker, A. (2010). "Virtue as Mastery in Early Confucianism," *Journal of Religious Ethics* 38(3): 404–428.

Stanley, J. (2011). *Know How* (Oxford: Oxford University Press).

Stanley, J. and Williamson, T. (2001). "Knowing How," *Journal of Philosophy* 98(8): 411–444.

Staudinger, U. (2010). "Wisdom," in I. Weiner and W. Craighead (eds.), *Corsini Encyclopedia of Psychology*, Vol. 4 (New York: Wiley), pp. 1860–1863.

Sternberg, R. (1985). "Implicit Theories of Intelligence, Creativity, and Wisdom," *Journal of Personality and Social Psychology* 49: 607–627.

Sternberg, R. (1998). "A Balance Theory of Wisdom," *Review of General Psychology* 2: 347–365.

Sternberg, R. (2001). "Why Schools Should Teach for Wisdom: The Balance Theory of Wisdom in Educational Settings," *Educational Psychologist* 36(4): 227–245.

Sternberg, R. (2003). *Wisdom, Intelligence, and Creativity Synthesized* (Cambridge: Cambridge University Press).

Sternberg, R. and Glück, J. (2019). "Why Is Wisdom Such an Obscure Field of Inquiry and What Can and Should Be Done about It?," in R. Sternberg and J. Glück (eds.), *The Cambridge Handbook of Wisdom* (Cambridge: Cambridge University Press), pp. 783–795.

Stichter, M. (2007). "Ethical Expertise: The Skill Model of Virtue," *Ethical Theory and Moral Practice* 10: 183–194.

Stichter, M. (2011). "Virtues, Skills, and Right Action," *Ethical Theory and Moral Practice* 14: 73–86.

Stichter, M. (2016). "Practical Skills and Practical Wisdom in Virtue," *Australasian Journal of Philosophy* 94(3): 435–448.

Stichter, M. (2018). *The Skillfulness of Virtue: Improving Our Moral and Epistemic Lives* (Cambridge: Cambridge University Press).

Swartwood, J. (2013). "Wisdom as an Expert Skill," *Ethical Theory and Moral Practice* 16: 511–528.

Swartwood, J. and Tiberius, V. (2011). "Wisdom Revisited: A Case Study in Normative Theorizing," *Philosophical Explorations* 14(3): 277–295.

Swartwood, J. and Tiberius, V. (2019). "Philosophical Foundations of Wisdom," in R. Sternberg and J. Glück (eds.), *The Cambridge Handbook of Wisdom* (Cambridge: Cambridge University Press), pp. 10–39.

Tiberius, V. (2000). *Deliberation about the Good: Justifying What We Value* (New York: Garland Publishing).

Tiberius, V. (2008). *The Reflective Life: Living Wisely with Our Limits* (Oxford: Oxford University Press).

Tsai, C. (2011a). "Linguistic Know-How: The Limits of Intellectualism," *Theoria* 77(1): 71–86.

Tsai, C. (2011b). "The Metaepistemology of Knowing-How," *Phenomenology and the Cognitive Sciences* 10(4): 541–556.

Tsai, C. (2014). "The Structure of Practical Expertise," *Philosophia* 42(2): 539–554.

Tsai, C. (2016). "Ethical Expertise and the Articulacy Requirement," *Synthese* 193(7): 2035–2052.

Tsai, C. (2020). "Phronesis and Techne: The Skill Model of Wisdom Defended," *Australasian Journal of Philosophy* 98(2): 234–247.

Tsai, C. (2022a). "Practical Wisdom, Well-Being, and Success," *Philosophy and Phenomenological Research* 104(3): 606–622.

Tsai, C. (2022b). "Beyond Intuitive Know-How," *Phenomenology and the Cognitive Sciences*. https://doi.org/10.1007/s11097-022-09851-5.

Tsai, C. (2022c). "Habit: A Rylean Conception," *Philosophies* 7(2): 45.

Whitcomb, D. (2011). "Wisdom," in S. Bernecker and D. Pritchard (eds.), *Routledge Companion to Epistemology* (London: Routledge), pp. 95–105.

Wiggins, D. (1975–1976). "Deliberation and Practical Reason," *Proceedings of the Aristotelian Society* 76: 29–51.

Yang, S. and Intezari, A. (2019). "Non-Western Lay Conceptions of Wisdom," in R. Sternberg and J. Glück (eds.), *The Cambridge Handbook of Wisdom* (Cambridge: Cambridge University Press), pp. 429–452.

Zagzebski, L. (2017). *Exemplarist Moral Theory* (Oxford: Oxford University Press).

Acknowledgments

I thank several publishers for granting permission to use parts of my previously published works. Springer Nature permitted use of material from "Ethical Expertise and the Articulacy Requirement," *Synthese*, 193(7) (July 2016), pp. 2035–2052. Taylor & Francis permitted use of material from "Phronesis and Techne: The Skill Model of Wisdom Defended," *Australasian Journal of Philosophy*, 98 (2) (2020), pp. 234–247. John Wiley & Sons permitted use of material from "Practical Wisdom, Well-Being, and Success," *Philosophy and Phenomenological Research*, 104(3) (May 2022), pp. 606–622. I am grateful to Professor Stephen Hetherington for inviting me to write this Element and for giving me the opportunity to develop the wisdom-as-skill thesis in a systematic way. I am also grateful to the Cambridge University Press anonymous referees for their extremely valuable comments and suggestions on earlier manuscripts. This work was supported by the Ministry of Science and Technology, Taiwan (MOST 109-2410-H-001-097-MY3 and 109-2410-H-001-090-MY3).

Epistemology

Stephen Hetherington
University of New South Wales, Sydney

Stephen Hetherington is Professor Emeritus of Philosophy at the University of New South Wales, Sydney. He is the author of numerous books including *Knowledge and the Gettier Problem* (Cambridge University Press, 2016), and *What Is Epistemology?* (Polity, 2019), and is the editor of, most recently, *Knowledge in Contemporary Epistemology* (with Markos Valaris: Bloomsbury, 2019), and *What the Ancients Offer to Contemporary Epistemology* (with Nicholas D. Smith: Routledge, 2020). He was the Editor-in-Chief of the *Australasian Journal of Philosophy* from 2013 until 2022.

About the Series

This Elements series seeks to cover all aspects of a rapidly evolving field including emerging and evolving topics such as these: fallibilism; knowinghow; self-knowledge; knowledge of morality; knowledge and injustice; formal epistemology; knowledge and religion; scientific knowledge; collective epistemology; applied epistemology; virtue epistemology; wisdom. The series will demonstrate the liveliness and diversity of the field, pointing also to new areas of investigation.

Cambridge Elements ☰

Epistemology

Elements in the Series

A full series listing is available at: www.cambridge.org/EEPI

CPSIA information can be obtained
at www.ICGtesting.com
Printed in the USA
BVHW050836250123
657061BV00016B/154

9 781009 222891